Accounting for Managers

An introduction to
financial and management accounting

3rd Edition

ENRICO ULIANA
BCom (Hons) MCom CA(SA)

DANNY MARCUS
BCom (Hons) CA(SA)

Juta & Co, Ltd

First Published in 1982 as
A BUSINESSMAN'S GUIDE TO FINANCIAL AND MANAGEMENT ACCOUNTING

Second Edition 1985
Reprinted Third Edition 1990

© Juta & Co, Ltd 1985
PO Box 14373, Kenwyn 7790

Cover: Joy Wrench
Cartoons: Wayne Osmond

ACKNOWLEDGEMENT
The authors wish to thank Mark Nigrini for his assistance in setting the questions for this book.

ISBN 0 7021 2359 5

PRINTED AND BOUND IN THE REPUBLIC OF SOUTH AFRICA
BY THE RUSTICA PRESS (PTY) LTD, NDABENI, CAPE
D1941

Preface

As with most disciplines, accounting is littered with jargon. Jargon is nothing more than a shorthand form of communication designed to confound and impress people outside any particular discipline. This explains why a surgeon may tell you that he will perform an incision just below your diaphragm when what he means is that he will have to slice open your belly.

This book is intended to clear some of the mystery surrounding financial and management accounting so that non-accountants may find it easier to communicate with accountants and seem knowledgeable when discussing matters such as ratio analysis (carving up a statement of affairs to see what is going on) or capital budgeting (deciding whether or not to embark on a project).

We hope that business people as well as students will find this book useful. This book is not intended to be an exhaustive reference to all aspects of financial and management accounting but we hope it will lead to understanding the key principles and serve as a foundation to any further study of the aspects discussed.

A word of warning—a little knowledge is a dangerous thing and just as you would probably consult a doctor when you have a pain in the stomach so that he may determine its cause, we hope that this book will alert you to those situations where a professional adviser should be called upon.

Our intention in writing this book was to enable you to communicate effectively within our discipline.

ENRICO ULIANA
DANNY MARCUS
Cape Town/Sydney
January 1990

Contents

1 A Brief History of Accounting

Accounting has developed as society's needs for the basis of recording commercial transactions have developed. As commercial transactions have become more numerous and more complex, accounting has had to change to cope with increasing complexities. In its earliest form accounting was simply a verbal report of transactions undertaken by somebody with a stewardship function on behalf of another person whose property was under their care. Now vast sums of money in diverse areas are controlled by relatively few people for the benefit of, sometimes, hundreds of thousands of investors. The need to record on a sophisticated basis has therefore arisen.

In 1494 Frater Luca Paciola wrote a treatise on mathematics. In this book he devoted a chapter to the principles of double entry bookkeeping. These basic principles of double entry bookkeeping have not been changed since and no matter how complex or involved accounting transactions and their underlying data may be, there has been no departure from these basic rules. This will become plain as we progress through the various topics in this book. These principles are fundamental to all forms of bookkeeping whether they be recorded by manual, mechanical or computerised means and we will deal with them in the following chapter. Even though we now live in the computer age where computers play such an important role in our lives and where the use of cash as an exchange commodity is being reduced by the growing popularity of credit cards, the centuries-old double entry bookkeeping system is still the underlying basis for the recording of all transactions. Many predictions have been made on expected developments in the computer field, particularly on the recording of commercial transactions. One of these predictions is rather interesting. It is expected that at some time in the near future all that will be required for a transaction is a card, perhaps in the form of a credit card, which a shopper would present to a merchant on completion of a transaction. This card would be inserted by the merchant into a card reader, the relevant amounts encoded and the customer's bank account will be reduced by the amount just spent, whereas the merchant's bank account would be increased, thus achieving an automatic change in the two parties' records. In addition, the merchant's records could be amended to take into account reduction of stock and the financial records suitably changed to record the result of this transaction, cumulatively with all others to date. If the customer is in business his records may also be immediately updated — recording that he now holds certain items of stock which he has bought — and his financial records would also be suitably updated on a cumulative basis. Even in the case of a fully integrated system such as the one just described the basic principles of double entry bookkeeping would still be applied in recording the various transactions which take place.

THE NEED FOR FINANCIAL RECORDS

Financial records are required in order to provide a basis from which to prepare financial reports to meet the information requirements of various different groups of people. Some considerable research has been done in this area. The results of this research are often published in the form of guidelines or recommendations which may be issued by accounting bodies in various countries. Some of this research has been concerned with determining who needs information and for what purposes. The following are the chief users of financial information:

(i) **Management.** Management requires information of a financial (and non-financial) nature to keep track of what is happening within a business entity for planning, control and decision-making purposes. This implies that management requires information in more detail than would normally be made publicly available.

(ii) **The owners.** The owners of the business entity, who may or may not be the management, need financial information to assess how effective management has been and to determine their future investment in the business.

(iii) **The suppliers of loan capital.** Suppliers of loan capital need financial information about the entity in order to ascertain whether they should advance money or require repayment of the amounts which they have advanced, as well as to determine the financial security of any advances which they may have made to the entity.

(iv) **Government authorities.** Government authorities require information about the entity to determine any taxes due or for the purposes of collecting statistical information for forward planning and, in some cases, to determine the position of the entity relative to any legislation which may be in effect.

(v) **Employees.** Employees of an entity could be said to require information regarding the entity employing them to determine the likelihood of their jobs being available in future or the financial stability of the company promising them retirement benefits, and perhaps, to acquire information for bargaining purposes on salary increases.

(vi) **Customers and suppliers.** Customers require information regarding the entity to assess whether their source of supply will continue in the future. Suppliers of goods and services to the entity would also require similar information to see whether the entity is going to require their goods and services in the future.

(vii) **Competitors.** Competitors would naturally want to know as much as possible about the entity but, as we shall see later in this chapter when we deal with internal versus external reporting requirements, the entity does not provide detailed information to all who may seek it.

(viii) **The general public.** Special interest groups within the general public also have a need for information about the entity which may not necessarily be of a financial nature, but is of relevance to gauge whether the social impact of the entity is material on society as a whole.

There is thus a wide and sometimes divergent need for information about an entity's activities and much of this information is required in a financial form. The financial form of reporting is this book's chief concern.

TYPES OF BUSINESS ENTITIES

Before we can deal with the question of how financial information is recorded it is necessary to consider the various types of business entities for which financial information may be required.

(i) **The Sole Trader**

The sole trader is a person who starts a business on his own. To do this he needs capital and the profit, hopefully, or any ensuing loss would respectively increase or decrease the amount of capital which the sole trader has in his business. The entire risk of loss of the business and, conversely, the entire profit of the business would be for the cost or the benefit of the sole trader. He has no protection against creditors in the event of business failure. Should the business fail it is not only the business assets which would be claimed by the persons who have advanced funds to the sole trader. If the sole trader's business assets do not satisfy the claims of all creditors, that is, if they are not worth sufficient to meet all the amounts owing, then the sole trader's personal assets such as his house, his motor car, etc. may have to be sold to pay all the amounts owing. For accounting purposes we record that the sole trader's business is an entity apart from the sole trader himself, but from a legal viewpoint the sole trader has all his personal assets at risk should the business fail.

(ii) **The Partnership**

The partnership is similar to the sole trader particularly with regard to the liability to outside sources of finance. The partners supply either capital to the business or in some cases their particular specialised abilities. The profits or losses are shared among the partners on an agreed basis. Like the sole trader, the partnership is recorded for financial reporting purposes as an entity distinct from the partners themselves. Legally, should the partnership business fail, the partners' personal assets could be attached in order to meet any obligations which the partnership business itself is unable to satisfy. In other words, in the case of the partnership, as with the sole trader, there is no limitation of liability which, as we shall see, exists with a business entity in the form of a company. A point to note with regard to a partnership is that all partners are jointly and severally liable for the debts of the partnership. This means that should one partner's personal assets be insufficient to meet his share of the obligations of the partnership, the other partners' assets can be sold beyond their proportionate liabilities in terms of the original partnership agreement. The law in South Africa limits the number of members in a partnership to a total of 20. There is a form of partnership, not often used, where provided due public notice has been given, the liability of a partner can be limited with regard to the general public. In that case should the business fail, the remaining partners would have to meet the obligations which the partnership assets were unable to meet. This is known as a partnership en commandite.

(iii) **The Private Company**

The private company is a company where the number of shareholders is between 1 and 50. Here the shareholders of the company would put capital into the business by way of share capital. Once the share capital has been subscribed or paid for, then the Companies Act operates so that the liability of the shareholders is limited to the amount of the share capital. This means that should the company not be able to meet its obligations, persons who have advanced money to the company are only entitled to claim from the company itself and not from its shareholders who are, in fact, the owners of the company. This is known as limited liability. The company, not only for financial recording purposes, but also from the legal viewpoint, is considered to be an entity entirely distinct from its owners. At first sight it seems that, particularly in the small business environment, it would be more desirable to trade as a private company, instead of as a sole trader or as a partnership. However, because it is common knowledge that companies do have limited liability, in practice when funds are advanced to a private company, often those advancing funds require the shareholders to give personal guarantees. Then if the business fails the liability which the company cannot meet would devolve upon them in their personal capacities.

Another important attribute of a company as opposed to a partnership, is the question of perpetual succession. A partnership is not viewed as a legal entity distinct from the partners themselves. Should the membership of the partnership change then the partnership itself ceases to exist and the new partners start afresh in a new undertaking. Whereas, because a company is a legal persona distinct from the persons owning the shares, should the ownership of the shares change, the company itself will continue in existence. Being a legal persona a company can enter into all forms of contract that a real person can, excepting, of course, those of a strictly personal nature such as marriage or divorce. How then does a company, in fact, achieve this?

For a company to come into being it is required that the promoters of the company register memorandum and articles of association. These documents are in effect the publicly recorded basis on which the company undertakes to conduct its business. Once these have been registered, any change must also be registered so that any person conducting business with the company knows the basis upon which they will contract.

(iv) **The Public Company**

The public company is similar in many respects to the private company with one major exception and that is the membership. The number of shareholders is unlimited, but must be no less than seven. A public company can be listed or unlisted. A private company can never be listed. Being listed means that the company has met the various requirements of the Stock Exchange, which in South Africa is the Johannesburg Stock Exchange, and that its shares can be publicly traded on that Stock Exchange. However, we shall see when we deal with reporting requirements later in this chapter, that the public company has more reporting requirements than the private company. It should be noted that there are specific requirements regarding the manner in which a company is permitted to raise finance from the general public.

Companies, both public and private, by virtue of being legal persona, are subject to taxation in their own right. Taxation is currently levied on companies at a fixed rate for every rand of taxable profit which they earn. Individuals are taxed on a sliding scale which increases with increases in the amount of taxable profit which they earn. The income derived from a partnership or a sole trader is taxed in the hands of the partner as regards his share of the profit, or the sole trader as regards the profit earned in his business, at individual rates of tax. Whereas the company's shareholders are not taxed on the company's profits, but only on dividends or other payments the company may make to them. It is important in deciding whether to trade as a sole trader, a partnership or a company to have some idea of the expected level of taxable profits as the differing tax rates would be a consideration in deciding which form of business entity to use to conduct one's business.

(v) **Close Corporations**

A Close Corporation is a type of business entity which can be loosely described as a cross between a partnership and a private company. It may be formed by one to ten persons and is governed by the Close Corporations Act.

This type of entity is particularly suitable for a business that is owned by a few people who are actively involved in its operations.

While enjoying limited liability, the statutory obligations are less onerous than in the case of a company, e.g. no meetings are required. An audit is also not required, merely a statement by an accounting officer, however, it is probably advisable to have an audit for the satisfaction of moneylenders and revenue authorities.

A Close Corporation is taxed in much the same way as a private company. There are, however, certain differences, particularly with regard to dividends. The most important of these being that distributions to members (i.e. dividends) are not taxable in the hands of the members.

REPORTING REQUIREMENTS

The sole trader has no legislated reporting requirements but information pertaining to the profit or loss made by the sole trader is required by the fiscal authorities in order to levy taxation. Certain government departments such as the Department of Statistics may require information for statistical or other purposes, but the reporting requirements themselves are not prescribed by legislation. Similarly, in the case of a partnership there are no legislated reporting requirements. The only reporting requirements are those which the partners themselves may prescribe in order to determine the profit or loss which has to be shared between them. The only requirement is that adequate information for the partners to be taxed on their share of the profit is needed. The Companies Act prescribes that all companies, whether they be private or public, are obliged to make their financial reports available to their shareholders in the form prescribed by the Companies Act. Section 286(3) of the Companies Act requires that the financial statements of a company be prepared in accordance with the requirements of the Fourth Schedule of that Act and with Generally Accepted Accounting Practice. (What consitutes Generally Accepted Accounting Practice will be dealt with in a later chapter.)

In addition, all companies are required to have their financial statements and records audited by independent auditors who are registered with the Public Accountants' and Auditors' Board. Private companies, therefore, would have to prepare financial statements in accordance with the requirements of the Companies Act. Public companies, which have the same requirement as private companies, are also obliged to issue interim reports, that is, half-yearly reports to their shareholders.

External Versus Internal Reporting

As we have seen, the only legislated external reporting requirements are those laid down by the Companies Act for private and public companies. It should also be noted that financial statements or reports must be prepared in accordance with the requirements of Section 286(3) of the Companies Act. When considering users of financial reports, we noted that competitors would naturally like to have as much information as possible about other businesses in their field, this has been recognised in the reporting requirements for the Companies Act, which limit the information that must be supplied. Sensitive information which may enable competitors, for example, to know by how much the company is marking up its goods, would not be revealed in financial statements which are prepared to meet the minimum requirements of the Companies Act. Internally, reporting requirements are quite different as the management of the company would need to have information pertaining to all aspects of the company's business for them to manage effectively. It is this area of financial information with which this book is chiefly concerned and which constitutes Management Accounting. We shall, however, in Chapter 3 be dealing with the format of External Financial Reports. They are relevant when one is examining the financial statements of a company without access to its internal information. This limited information in external financial reports may be all that is available to assess the financial position of a company. We therefore need to examine the nature and type of information which would be supplied.

QUESTIONS

In each of the following cases indicate whether the fact/s stated are true or false:

(a) Society has always tailored its needs to accommodate the degree of development in accounting.

(b) Computers have made the principles of double entry redundant.

(c) The general public cannot be considered as users of financial information as they have no interest in the actions of business enterprises.

(d) Sole traders take the full risk of business failure in their personal capacities, whereas there is no such risk attached to the shareholders of companies.

(e) Public companies are always listed on recognised stock exchanges.

(f) While in theory there is no limit to the number of shareholders in a public company there is ultimately a limit which is a function of the number of shares a company has available to issue at any point in time.

(g) Internal management reporting requirements are not legislated for insofar as their form and content is concerned.

(h) Competitors should be provided with the same information as is made available to management.

(i) It is absolutely essential to be able to communicate in the jargon used in a discipline so as to be able to impress and mystify others.

2 Basic Book-keeping

Before we examine the principle of double entry and the recording of transactions, terminology commonly used should be considered.

Income—is reflected by amounts recorded when goods are supplied or services are rendered to others e.g. sales of goods supplied, fees for services rendered, interest received from making funds available to others.

Expenses—are reflected by amounts recorded for goods consumed and services received, e.g. stock consumed, rent for use of premises, interest paid for use of funds.

Liabilities—Amounts owed to suppliers of funds, e.g. loans, trade creditors, bank overdrafts.

Assets—Items owned or amounts due by others, e.g. fixed property, stock and other movables, trade debtors, cash resources.

Profit/Loss—The difference between income and expenditure. If income is greater than expenditure there is a profit and the converse is a loss.

Capital—The difference between assets and liabilities. If assets exceed liabilities this would be equivalent to the amount an entity is worth to its owners. Should the reverse apply this would be equivalent to the loss which may have to be borne by either the owners or suppliers of finance, depending on the legal form of the entity. However, you should note that financial statements generally record assets and liabilities at their historic cost. This is dealt with in Chapter 4, under Accounting Conventions.

PRINCIPLES OF DOUBLE ENTRY

Accountants are known for their extreme conservatism, probably because they do everything twice. But this is not how the double entry system came about. Rather, it means that every financial transaction causes two equal reactions. For example, if you were to purchase a motor vehicle and pay for it in cash, two things would occur. Firstly, you would own a motor vehicle, and secondly, the amount of cash which you had would diminish by the amount used to buy the motor vehicle. The principle of double entry requires that these two components of each transaction always be recorded. You would therefore record what has actually occurred. The advantage is that because two reactions have occurred from the one transaction, and because they are both equal in amount, i.e. the purchase price of the motor vehicle is equal to the reduction of the cash you had, your books, assuming that no errors have occurred, and if they have been drawn up on the principle of double entry, must always balance. This arises because all transactions which you record would have been entered in terms of the two reactions resulting from any one transaction.

If we take a few examples of everyday transactions we can see how the aforegoing is applied.

Transactions	*Reactions*
1. The owner of the business opens a bank account and deposits R2 000 cash.	1a. The business has R2 000 in a bank account. b. The owner has R2 000 capital in the business.
2. Purchase of several items of stock for R500 cash.	2a. Stock, an asset, has been acquired for R500. b. Cash on hand, also an asset, has been reduced by R500.
3. Purchase of furniture and fittings for R800 cash.	3a. Fixtures and fittings, an asset has been acquired for R800. b. Cash, an asset, has been reduced by the purchase price of R800.
4. Purchase of a further R600 of stock from a creditor J. Bloggs.	4a. Stock, an asset, has been acquired for R600. b. J. Bloggs, a creditor and hence a liability, granted us credit and we have incurred a liability of R600.
5. Payment of R400 to J. Bloggs.	5a. The amount owing to J. Bloggs, a creditor and hence a liability, has been reduced by R400. b. Cash on hand, an asset, has been reduced by R400. (In other words we have reduced a liability and simultaneously reduced an asset.)

6. Sale of stock to C. Lark, credit granted to C. Lark. The stock was sold for R750 and cost us R400.

6(i)a. C. Lark now owes us R750.

(i)b. We need to note the fact that income has been earned in that we have made a sale of R750.

(ii)a. We have incurred an expense of R400, being the cost of stock which we have sold.

(ii)b. Stock on hand having been consumed has been reduced by R400. (In this case two transactions have occurred. Firstly, we have sold goods to C. Lark and secondly, we have consumed some of our stock.)

7. C. Lark pays us R300 on account.

7a. We now have a further R300 cash on hand, that is, our asset has increased by R300.

b. One of our other assets, i.e. C. Lark, our debtor, has been diminished in that C. Lark no longer owes us the R750, but has reduced the amount owing to us by R300 to a total outstanding of R450.

8. Rent of R75 paid.

8a. An expense of R75 for the use of premises has been incurred.

b. Cash, an asset, has been reduced by R75.

9. Wages of R135 paid.

9a. An expense of R135 for wages has been incurred.

b. Cash, an asset, has been reduced by R135.

We can thus see that for every transaction there would be two reactions which we would record.

The two reactions arising from every transaction have by convention been recorded either as debits or as credits. It is important at this stage to notice that the convention is as follows: debits are recorded on the left and credits are recorded on the right. The following items would be recorded as debits and credits:

Debit	Credit
Assets	Liabilities
Expenses	Income
Increases in assets	Increases in liabilities
Decreases in liabilities	Decreases in assets
Capital deficit	Capital surplus

It is quite easy to learn the above by h art and it is not a particularly long table. But it can be proved logically that if one accepts the first convention, namely that each transaction gives rise to two opposite reactions, and we then accept as a convention that income is recorded as a credit, it follows that because an expense is the opposite of income, and income is recorded as a credit, an expense must be recorded as a debit.

Let us take a simple example to illustrate the above:

	R
Sales	100
Expenses	60
Profit	40

We have said that we would accept as a convention that income (in this case sales) would be recorded as a credit. It follows that expenses being the opposite of income would be recorded as a debit, i.e.

	R	
Sales	100	credit
Expenses	60	debit
Profit	40	credit

The profit of R40 is, by simple arithmetic, a credit, and we must decide if this is in line with the table we have drawn up. Indeed it is, as profit is ultimately owed to the owners of a business and forms part of their capital. It can be regarded as an ultimate liability to the owners and should be recorded as a credit and it follows that assets, the opposite of liabilities, should be recorded as debits. Capital, ultimately owed by the business to its owners, is also recorded as a credit by the business. Of course capital is not a liability, of the business, this is just a convenient way of thinking about it. What we have just described may be summarised in the accounting equation which is that

Capital = Assets − Liabilities and by convention capital is a credit, the rest follows logically.

JOURNAL ENTRIES

Applying these conventions to the examples earlier in this chapter and recording them in the form referred to as journal entries, they would appear as follows for the reasons indicated:

Journal Entries	Debit	Credit	Reason
1. Bank	2 000		Asset
Capital		2 000	Capital
Capital introduced			
2. Stock	500		Asset
Bank		500	Reduction of asset
Stock purchased			
3. Furniture and fittings	800		Asset
Bank		800	Reduction of asset
Furniture and fittings purchased			
4. Stock	600		Asset
J. Bloggs/Trade creditors		600	Liability
Stock purchased on credit			
5. J. Bloggs/Trade creditors	400		Reduction of liability
Bank		400	Reduction of assets
Payment to J. Bloggs			
6i. C. Lark/Trade debtors	750		Asset
Sales		750	Income
Sale on credit			
6ii. Cost of sales	400		Expense
Stock		400	Reduction of asset
Stock consumed			
7. Bank	300		Asset
C. Lark/Trade debtors		300	Reduction of asset
Payment received from C. Lark			
8. Rent	75		Expense
Bank		75	Reduction of asset
Rent paid			
9. Wages	135		Expense
Bank		135	Reduction of asset
Wages paid			

TRIAL BALANCE

If you wished to establish how the business had fared at the end of these transactions, you would simply add and subtract all like items in the journal and draw up a listing of these in what is known as a trial balance.

TRIAL BALANCE

	Debits	Credits
Bank (2 000 − 500 − 800 − 400 + 300 − 75 − 135)	390	
Capital		2 000
Stock (500 + 600 − 400)	700	
Furniture and fittings	800	
J. Bloggs (600 − 400)		200
C. Lark (750 − 300)	450	
Sales		750
Cost of sales	400	
Rent	75	
Wages	135	
	R2 950	R2 950

This trial balance indicates that the transactions recorded are arithmetically correct, i.e. the total of the debits is equal to the total of the credits.

To establish how the business has fared, the amounts appearing in the trial balance can now be expressed by inserting the income and expenses in an income statement (which would show the results of transactions) and the assets, liabilities and capital in a balance sheet (which would show the financial position after the transactions).

INCOME STATEMENT

INCOME		
Sales		750
EXPENSES		
Cost of sales	400	
Rent	75	
Wages	135	
		610
Profit		R140*

BALANCE SHEET

Capital introduced	2 000
Profit	140*
	R2 140

ASSETS

Furniture and fittings	800
Stock	700
Bank	390
Trade debtors	450
	2 340

LIABILITIES

Trade creditors	200
	R2 140

* Note: As profits are ultimately owed to the owners or losses borne by them, profits are added or losses subtracted from capital.

The presentation of financial reports including the above will be dealt with fully later.

BOOKS OF ACCOUNT

The example dealt with, although containing few transactions when compared to the number that occur daily in even the smallest business, has generated a large number of journal entries to be condensed and presented in an acceptable format.

This problem is overcome in two broad areas: firstly, by the use of a nominal ledger and secondly, by the use of specialised journals referred to as books of prime entry.

Instead of adding up all the journal entries as done in the example, a page is allocated to each asset, liability, expense, income or capital account in the nominal ledger. These are called nominal accounts.

All items for each account are recorded in the ledger in the specific page which is divided into debit and credit entries, and is thus a summary of transactions recorded in the journal affecting that account.

A typical ledger page would appear as follows:

STOCK							68
19x0				19x0			
Jan 3	Purchases	J11	500	Jan 15	Cost of sales	J11	400
Jan 20	Purchases	J11	600	Jan 31	Balance	c/d	700
			1 100				1 100
19x0							
Feb 1	Balance	b/d	700				

Manually produced ledgers take many forms but in general they are much like the example shown here. These principles still apply in computerised systems although the format of the ledger may be somewhat different. Specialised journals are used to remove the repetition of entries of a similar type. The books of prime entry and their function are generally the following:

Book of Prime Entry	Function
Nominal journal	To record non-repetitive type transactions
Purchases journal	To record credit purchases
Cash book	To record transactions with the bank
Sales journal	To record credit sales
Petty cash book	To record minor cash transactions

A further refinement which is generally found is the use of subsidiary ledgers. These ledgers are used to avoid cluttering up the nominal ledger with numerous personal accounts for individual debtors or creditors. The subsidiary ledger is represented in the nominal ledger by a control account for each subsidiary ledger in use. The balance on the control account will be equal to the total of all individual accounts in the subsidiary ledger.

THE RELATIONSHIP OF THE BOOKS OF ACCOUNTS

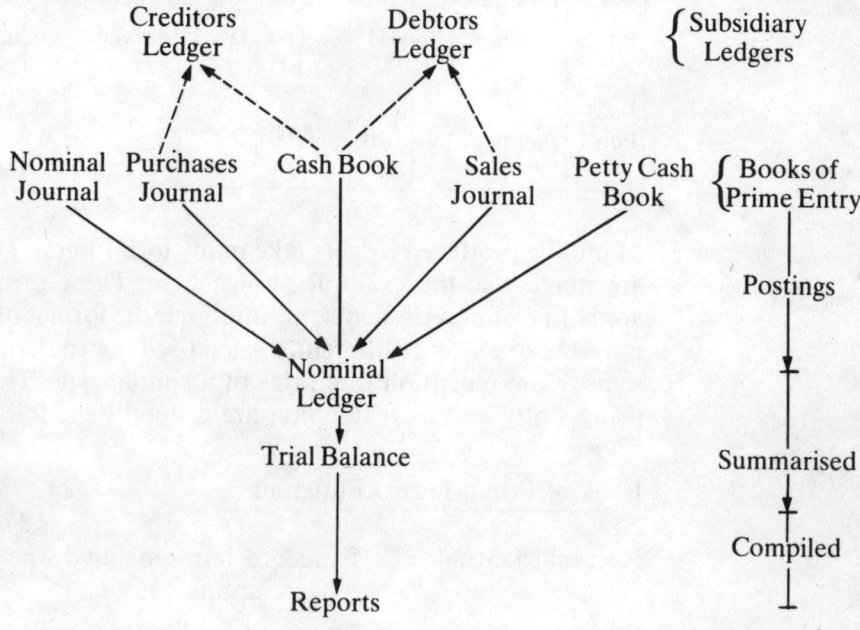

In addition to removing the repetitive nature of recording all transactions in the nominal ledger, the use of specialised journals facilitates the division of the book-keeping functions among several people.

Once the books of prime entry are completed and the amounts in these books posted to the nominal ledger, a trial balance may be extracted. A list of the balances on the individual accounts in the nominal ledger is made. The total of the debit balances and the total of the credit balances will equal each other if the books have been kept with arithmetic accuracy.

At this point it should be noted that a balanced trial balance does not indicate that the books have been accurately prepared, as a posting to the wrong account does not affect the arithmetical accuracy. The correctness of the individual accounts may be verified in numerous ways e.g. the rent account should generally show one payment per month, the creditors control must agree with the total of the creditors' ledger, and each creditor's account should be reconciled to the statement of account from the particular creditor.

The trial balance is merely the result of routine book-keeping and requires adjustment for items which are not the result of transactions of a routine nature e.g. depreciation and other internal adjustments.

These items together with the figures on the trial balance are utilised to compile the various reports. It is important that the adjustments are recorded via the journal so that the books reflect all transactions and adjustments.

The preparation of a trial balance as laid out in this chapter seems very simple, which is as it should be. However, the number of bald book-keepers who have torn their hair out over trial balances may suggest otherwise.

QUESTIONS

2.1 In each of the following cases indicate whether the fact/s stated are true or false:

    (a) Items of income include bank overdrafts.

    (b) The term double entry means that two books are always used for all entries.

    (c) Cash is an asset and is therefore always a debit.

    (d) Because cash is an asset any entries effecting cash can always only be debits.

    (e) Trial Balances are always easy to produce without any errors.

2.2 You are required to show the journal entries to record the following transactions in the books of J. Student:

(a) J. Student manages to con the bank to grant a loan of R2 000.

(b) J. Student decides it is appropriate to draw some of the money before the bank changes its mind and cashes a cheque for R250.

(c) J. Student decides to buy a copy of this book at its very reasonable price of R75 and pays cash.

(d) Rent on digs for January amounting to R300 is paid by cheque.

(e) S. Hopkeeper allows J. Student to buy stationery amounting to R125 on credit.

(f) The first interest payment of R25 is charged to J. Student's account by the bank.

(g) J. Student pays R50 to S. Hopkeeper on account.

(h) J. Student played back-gammon in the students union and lost R65 to R. Ugvark.

What is the balance in J. Student's bank account after the above transactions have been processed?

Assuming that J. Student has not lied about the amount lost while playing back-gammon, how much cash does J. Student have left?

3 Financial Statement Preparation

Financial statements are a basis from which to work for those who wish to make decisions regarding a particular business entity. In Chapter One the various users of financial information were discussed and they include:

Management
Owners
Suppliers of loan capital
Government authorities
Employees
Customers
Competitors, and
Special interest groups within the general public

Broadly speaking a set of financial statements represents the results of a business' operations i.e. the profit or loss for a period of time, as well as the financial position of the business at the end of that period.

The profit or loss of the business is exhibited in various statements depending on the activities of the business. These statements are 'the income statement', 'the trading statement' and 'the manufacturing statement'. Every business will prepare an income statement which is the summarisation of the profit or loss for the period. In the case of companies involved in trading activities (i.e. the buying and selling of goods) a trading statement will also be prepared. A manufacturing business will prepare a manufacturing statement in addition to the statements mentioned previously. The trading statement will show the results of the trading operations (known as gross profit) while the manufacturing statement will show the cost of the goods manufactured.

A balance sheet is a report which shows the financial position of an entity at a particular time.

TRIAL BALANCE TO BALANCE SHEET

These statements and their preparation from a trial balance are illustrated in the following example:

JAMS MANUFACTURING Dr Cr

TRIAL BALANCE AT 31 DECEMBER 02

	Dr	Cr
Auditors' remuneration	2 000 *Expenditure*	
Advertising	3 000 *Exp*	
Cash discounts—allowed	1 000 *Exp*	
—received		2 000 *Exp*
Consumable stores	6 000 *Exp*	
Creditors		50 000 *Liab*
Capital 1.1.02 *shareholders*		52 000 *Liab*
Debtors	65 000 *Assets*	
Depreciation—plant and machinery	5 000 *Exp*	
—motor vehicles	4 000	
—office equipment	1 000	
Drawings	20 000 *owners Equity*	
Electricity	8 000	
Plant and machinery, cost	54 000	
accumulated depreciation		10 000
Motor vehicles, cost	20 000	
accumulated depreciation		8 000
Office equipment, cost	6 000	
accumulated depreciation		2 000
Motor expenses	2 000	
Interest—loan	4 000	
—overdraft	1 000	
Bank overdraft		5 000
Printing and stationery	1 000	
Purchases—materials	45 000	
Rent—factory buildings	24 000	
—administration offices	6 000	
Salaries—administration	10 000	
—sales staff	9 000	
Sales		210 000
Stock 1.1.02—Materials	7 000 *ass*	
—Work in progress	3 000	
—Finished goods	23 000	
Repairs and maintenance		
—plant and machinery	3 000 *exp*	
Telephone and postage	2 000 *exp*	
Tost Trust – loan		45 000 *Liab*
Travel and entertainment	3 000 *Exp*	
Wages—direct	28 000	
—indirect	18 000	
	R384 000	R384 000

Stock on hand at 31.12.02 was

Material	8 000
Work in progress	4 000
Finished goods	18 000
	R30 000

Comments on the trial balance:

1. For illustrative purposes the balance sheet items (viz. assets, liabilities and capital) are in italics.

2. Fixed assets are consumed over their lifetime. This is recognised by treating a portion of the asset annually as an expense by way of depreciation. It may be expected that a debit would be passed to record the depreciation expense; the commensurate credit being deducted from the relevant asset account. However, to maintain a record of the original cost of the asset in the books of account, the credit is placed in an account for accumulated depreciation of the specific class of asset.

3. The figure of R30 000 noted at the bottom of the trial balance is an example of an adjustment made by pro-forma entry. This is a figure which was not included in the books of account at the time the trial balance was prepared but needs to be taken into account.

4. All the items contained in the trial balance and in the pro-forma entries can be traced to the various reports which follow. Items marked * have been derived simply by addition or subtraction.

JAMS MANUFACTURING

MANUFACTURING STATEMENT
FOR THE YEAR ENDED 31 DECEMBER 02

Materials		
Stock 1.1.02	7 000	
Purchases	45 000	
	52 000	
Less: Stock 31.12.02	8 000	
Material Usage		44 000*
Direct labour		28 000
Prime cost		72 000*

Manufacturing overheads
　　Consumable stores   6 000
　　Depreciaiton of plant and
　　　machinery   5 000
　　Electricity   8 000
　　Indirect labour   18 000
　　Rent   24 000
　　Repairs and maintenance of
　　　plant and machinery   3 000
　　 ────────
　　 64 000
　　 ────────
　　 136 000
Work in Progress 1.1.02   3 000
　　 ────────
　　 139 000
Less: Work in Progress 31.12.02   4 000
　　 ────────
Cost of manufacture   R135 000*
　　 ════════

Comments on the manufacturing statement:

1. The cost of materials used for the year is not only the cost of materials purchased, as this would not take into account the stock of materials on hand at the beginning and end of the year. The stock on hand at the beginning of the year together with the purchases made, comprises the material available for use. If the stock on hand at the end of the year is deducted from the material available for use this results in the cost of material used.

   This principle is equally applicable to work in progress at the beginning of the year and that which is incomplete at the end of the year.

   The figure for purchase of materials would include all costs associated with bringing the goods onto the premises.

2. Those expenses that are related to the manufacturing activities are charged to the manufacturing statement. The purpose of the manufacturing statement is to establish the cost of manufactured goods. This aspect is discussed in Chapter 6.

JAMS MANUFACTURING

TRADING STATEMENT
FOR THE YEAR ENDED 31 DECEMBER 02

Sales *or turnover*		210 000
Less: Cost of Sales		
Stock 1.1.02	23 000	
Cost of manufacture	135 000	
Goods available for sale	158 000*	
Less: stock 31.12.02	18 000	
		140 000
Gross profit		R70 000*

Comments on trading statement:

1. Notice that the cost of manufacture of R135 000 has been transferred from the manufacturing statement.
2. Note that the stocks of finished goods are taken into account in the determination of the cost of sales on the same basis as materials and work in progress in the manufacturing statement.
3. In the case of a non-manufacturing trading business the cost of manufacture would be replaced by purchases of goods for resale in the calculation of cost of sales. The figure for purchases would include all costs associated with bringing the goods onto the premises i.e. railage and carriage inwards, and after taking trade discount into account.

JAMS MANUFACTURING

INCOME STATEMENT
FOR THE YEAR ENDED 31 DECEMBER 02

Income		
Gross profit		70 000
Cash discounts received		2 000
		72 000
Less: Expenditure		
Administration		
Auditors' remuneration	2 000	
Depreciation of office equipment	1 000	
Printing and stationery	1 000	
Office rent	6 000	
Salaries	10 000	
Telephone and postages	2 000	
		22 000

Financial
  Cash discount allowed   1 000
  Interest on loan   4 000
  Interest on overdraft   1 000
                                                        6 000

Selling and Distribution
  Advertising   3 000
  Depreciation of motor
    vehicles   4 000
  Motor expenses   2 000
  Salaries and commission   9 000
  Travel and entertainment   3 000
                                                       21 000
                                                       49 000
Net income   23 000*

Comments on the income statement:

1. Notice that the gross profit of R70 000 has been transferred from the trading statement. In practice the trading and income statements are often combined, in the following manner:

JAMS MANUFACTURING

TRADING AND INCOME STATEMENT
FOR THE YEAR ENDED 31 DECEMBER 02

Sales   210 000
Less: Cost of Sales
  Stock 1.1.02   23 000
  Cost of manufacture   135 000
  Goods available for sale   158 000*
  Less: Stock 31.12.02   18 000
                                                             140 000
Gross profit   70 000*
Cash discounts received   2 000
                                                              72 000

Less: Expenditure
  Administration
  Accounting fees   2 000
  Depreciation of office equip-
    ment   1 000
  etc. . . .

2. As is often done in practice expenses have been listed under various headings for the sake of easy reference.

JAMS MANUFACTURING

BALANCE SHEET AT 31 DECEMBER 02

CAPITAL EMPLOYED
Capital

Balance 1.1.02	52 000	
Net income	23 000	
	75 000	
Less: Drawings	20 000	
Balance 31.12.02		55 000*
Long term liability		
Loan — Tost Trust		45 000
		R100 000

EMPLOYMENT OF CAPITAL

Fixed assets—book value (note 1)		60 000*
Current assets		
Stock (note 2)	30 000	
Debtors	65 000	
	95 000	
Current liabilities		
Creditors	50 000	
Overdraft	5 000	
	55 000	
Net current assets		40 000*
		R100 000

Notes to the balance sheet:

1. Fixed assets

	Cost	Accumulated depreciation	Book value
Plant and machinery	54 000	10 000	44 000
Motor vehicles	20 000	8 000	12 000
Office equipment	6 000	2 000	4 000
	R80 000	— R20 000 ≈	R60 000*

2. Stock

Ending →

Materials	8 000 ·
Work in progress	4 000 ·
Finished goods	18 000 ·
	R30 000

Comments on the balance sheet and the notes to the balance sheet:

1. The balance sheet is compiled at one point in time whereas the income statement and related documents are compiled for periods of time (in this case one year). The profit for the period is added to (or the loss deducted from) the capital balance at the beginning of the period and the amounts withdrawn by the owners are deducted from this amount to arrive at the capital balance (or net worth of the business to its owners) at the balance sheet date. In other words the capital at the beginning and end of the year is linked by way of the trading results for the year, adjusted for withdrawals or additions of capital.

2. Long term liabilities are those which are due for payment more than one year after balance sheet date and are conventionally separated and disclosed as shown here.

   The above balance sheet indicates that Jams Manufacturing is financed to the extent of R55 000 by its owners and to the extent of R45 000 by suppliers of long term debt.

3. Current assets are normally listed in reverse order of liquidity. This means that assets least near cash are listed first. The converse applies to current liabilities.

4. The situation where current assets exceed current liabilities is described as either net current assets or working capital. If current liabilities exceed current assets this is described as net current liabilities or working capital deficit.

5. Notes to the balance sheet or the other documents discussed are often used to avoid cluttering up the statements with too much detail.

6. Debtors and creditors are frequently referred to as accounts receivable and accounts payable respectively.

COMPARATIVE FIGURES

In practice the figures for the preceding period are also published along with the current period figures so that comparisons may be made.

The above format of financial statements is produced for internal use. In the next chapter we shall deal with the legal requirements regarding the financial information which companies must publish. The detailed information discussed in this chapter would be for the use of management who may, if they feel it necessary, disclose it on a restricted basis to parties such as their bank. The authorities may require the information for tax assessment purposes.

These comments should not be misconstrued as meaning that different financial statements are specially prepared for different people!

QUESTIONS

3.1 In each of the following cases indicate whether the fact/s stated are true or false:

(a) An income statement is prepared to report on the financial position of a business at a specific point in time.

(b) A manufacturing business will never prepare a trading statement.

(c) Accumulated depreciation is shown separately on a balance sheet so as to be able to show the original cost of fixed assets.

(d) Stock on hand at the beginning and end of a reporting period is taken into account so as to derive the amount of stock items consumed during the period.

(e) There are no conventions applied in financial statement preparations. This is done on purpose to make life easier for those preparing such statements and it is left to the users of the reports to figure out what is going on.

3.2 Using the following trial balance prepare the financial statements of Devries Limited for the year ended 30 June, 03.

	Debits	Credits
Accumulated profit, July 1		67 000
Advertising	795	
Annual duty	65	
Audit fees	8 500	
Accruals		2 350
Bad debts	6 700	
Bank	8 700	
Buildings, at cost	220 000	
Buildings, accumulated depreciation		160 000
Carriage inwards	7 800	
Commission received		11 285
Creditors, trade		67 800
Creditors, long term loans		124 000
Cash	5 600	
Debtors	45 000	
Discount received		2 370
Discount paid	3 330	
Electricity and water	5 600	
Equipment, at cost	143 000	
Equipment, accumulated depreciation		56 700
Fittings, at cost	14 600	
Fittings, accumulated depreciation		3 600
Hire of equipment	7 680	
Insurance	9 500	
Interest paid	6 735	
Land, at cost	156 000	
Maintenance, factory	15 600	
Maintenance, office	700	
Motor vehicle hire: delivery	7 850	
sales	5 500	
Postage and telephone	9 500	
Purchases, materials	360 000	
Rent: Factory	87 000	
Office	7 650	
Sales	7 800	
Salaries and Wages: Factory	144 900	
Office	98 900	
Sales staff	127 000	
Sales		1 090 500
Share capital, ordinary shares		50 000
Stock 1 July: Materials	45 000	
Work in progress	12 600	
Finished goods	56 000	
	R1 635 605	R1 635 605

NOTES

1. Depreciation is provided at the following rates:
   Buildings   15% per annum on the straight line basis
   Fittings   10% per annum on the straight line basis
   Equipment 20% per annum on the reducing balance basis

2. Stock on hand at 30 June was:

Materials	56 700
Work in progress	5 750
Finished goods	36 850

3. There are no taxes payable.

4. Devries Ltd has decided to declare a dividend of 40% of net profit.

4 External Reporting Requirements

Internal reporting is intended for the use of management in the day to day running of a business. This implies that internal reports will contain information which may be superfluous to the needs of external users; moreover internal reports may contain confidential information which no business would willingly make public.

In the case of a company there is a statutory duty to report to the shareholders, who are its owners and have a right to the limited information.

Statute generally requires that the Annual Financial Statements of a company shall fairly present the financial position and results of the operations and be produced in accordance with Generally Accepted Accounting Practice (GAAP) and disclose at least the minimum prescribed.

STATUTORY REQUIREMENTS

Company legislation normally details those items which must be disclosed in annual financial statements. The 4th Schedule of the Companies Act details the minimum disclosure requirement for South African Companies.

Examples of items which may be required to be disclosed are:

(a) Directors' report
  —Nature of the company's business
  —Details of directors
  —Comment on the results of the business

(b) Balance sheet
  —Cost and accumulated depreciation of fixed assets
  —Secured liabilities
  —Stocks

(c) Income statement
  —Turnover
  —Interest paid
  —Depreciation

(d) Statement of source and application of funds
  —Cash flows from trading operations
  —Dividends
  —Changes in working capital

(e) Notes to the financial statements
   —Basis of valuation of stock
   —Details of land and buildings in certain circumstances
   —Details of share capital

The income statement in Chapter 3 may be presented as follows so as to comply with statutory requirements.

JAMS LIMITED

INCOME STATEMENT

FOR THE YEAR ENDED 31-12-02

Turnover		R210 000
Net income after charging the items		
detailed hereunder		R23 000
Auditors' remuneration	2 000	
Depreciation	10 000	
Interest paid	5 000	

Compare this to the income statement in Chapter 3 which was prepared for internal use. It is apparent that the details of items such as cost of sales, gross profit and other expenses are not made available to external users.

GENERALLY ACCEPTED ACCOUNTING PRACTICE

There are various areas where, depending upon the accounting basis selected, several results can be obtained from the same set of data. An illustration of this is contained in the following chapter which deals with the valuation of stock.

The problem is in determining which basis would result in a fair presentation. To this end accounting bodies in many countries have engaged in research to determine what constitutes Generally Accepted Accounting Practice (GAAP) in several of the problem areas. These bodies have issued statements of what, in their opinion, constitutes GAAP. These statements lay down the basis of accounting which may, in some countries, have to be adopted in external reports to comply with statutory requirements.

A company's auditor may have a statutory duty to give an opinion on the annual financial statements. If the auditor feels that the financial statements do not comply with the relevant requirements there may be an obligation to make this clear by qualifying the audit report. Companies prefer to avoid a qualification in the auditor's report so as not to cast doubt upon their reported results. This in itself is a major contributor to compliance with GAAP where applicable.

ACCOUNTING CONVENTIONS

There are certain conventions to which most accounting bodies subscribe. A user of financial statements may assume that the following conventions have been applied unless otherwise stated.

Going-concern—Financial statements are prepared on the assumption that the business will continue to trade for the foreseeable future (unless there is concrete evidence to the contrary) and asset values are recorded in this context and not, for example, written down to liquidation values.

Matching—Income and expenses are matched to accord with the period to which they relate. For example, sales are recorded when goods are delivered, not when the cash is subsequently received.

Prudence—All foreseeable losses are provided for, whereas income is recognised only in the period in which it is realised. In the event of conflict, prudence takes precedence over matching.

Consistency—Like items are treated in the same manner from period to period.

Historic cost—Assets and liabilities are recorded at their historic cost. Any departure from this is adequately noted, for example where assets have been revalued to replacement cost.

CHANGING PRICE LEVELS

Most companies have and may continue to experience significant inflation. It is widely recognised that this phenomenon has a substantial impact on the distributability of reported profits. Financial statements prepared in accordance with the historic cost covention do not take into account the effects of changing price levels. This can be illustrated by means of the following example:

Consider the case of a trading business which buys an item of stock with its initial capital of R10 and sells this item of stock for R15, by which time the replacement cost of the item has risen from R10 to R12. Recording these transactions immediately after the sale and repurchase of the stock item, the financial statements, using historic cost accounting, would be as follows:

INCOME STATEMENT

		R
Sales		15
Cost of sales		
Purchases (10 + 12)	22	
Closing stock	12	
		10
Profit		5

BALANCE SHEET

		R
Capital		
Initial capital	10	
Profit	5	
		15
Current assets		
Stock (FIFO)*	12	
Cash (15 − 12)	3	
		15

* FIFO (first in–first out) see Chapter 5.

It can be seen that the apparently distributable profit of R5 is at variance with the cash on hand of R3, as the accounting procedures have neglected to cater for the increased replacement cost of the stock.

Much research has been done into the problem of accounting for increasing price levels. Several solutions have been proposed by various accounting bodies and much dispute exists as to the most appropriate solution.

The basic similarity in the proposals is that of charging the value to the business of the items consumed at the time of their consumption. If this were applied to the above example the financial statements would be as follows:

CURRENT COST INCOME STATEMENT

		R
Sales		15
Cost of sales (as before)	10	
Cost of sales adjustment	2	
		12
Operating profit		3
Holding gain		2
Total profit		5

This income statement illustrates that during a period of rising prices the business has had a gain of R2 due to an appreciation in the value of its stock holding. The business has earned an operating profit of R3 by selling an item worth R12 (which it needs to replace to continue in business) for R15.

CURRENT COST BALANCE SHEET

		R
Capital		
Initial capital		10
Operating profit		3
Holding gain		2
		15
Current assets		
Stock		12
Cash		3
		15

Notice that the reported distributable profit is now equal to the cash on hand.

This example has ignored the problems associated with fixed assets and purchases and sales on credit but illustrates the basic principle.

This subject has been hotly debated at various times. However, a cynical observer may feel that the intensity of concern regarding the problem of accounting for inflation is directly correlated to the rate of inflation and its degree of impact on reported results experienced in a particular country at that time.

QUESTIONS

4.1 In each of the following cases indicate whether the fact/s stated are true or false:

(a) A distinction is made between internal and external reporting so as to limit the amount of confidential information which is made public.

(b) A recipient of financial statements prepared specifically for external use would normally be able to determine sensitive information such as gross profit ratios.

(c) A reference to GAAP means that the financial statements have been prepared with no regard to compliance with standards of reporting.

(d) The question of Current Value accounting has not been satisfactorily resolved and there is no general agreement as to how the effects of inflation on reported results should be accounted for in financial statements.

(e) Financial statements prepared in accordance with the historic cost convention are adequate for all circumstances.

4.2 Prepare two financial statements using the following information, one set using the historic cost convention, the other by applying current values.

	Debits	Credits
Purchases	78 000	
Cash	4 000	
Sales		85 000
Expenses	12 500	
Capital		48 000
Fixed Assets	38 500	
	R133 000	R133 000

Stock on hand at 31.12.01 amounted to R8 000, at cost and had replacement value of R12 500.

The year ended 31.12.01 was Todd Ltd's first year of trading.

5 Stocks and Work in Progress

Stock is often one of the most significant assets which a business has and consequently even a small change in the value of the amount calculated may have a material effect on the reported results. The question of stock control is dealt with in Chapter 12.

A change in the value of stock may arise from:

1. An error in recording during the stock count
2. An error in calculation of the value
3. Adopting a different stock valuation policy.

It is this latter aspect which is the subject of this chapter.

METHODS OF VALUATION

FIFO

The most commonly used method is described as First In–First Out (FIFO). This method of valuation is based on the assumption that the oldest item of stock on hand is the first one used. Therefore the items remaining in stock are those most recently acquired. It is not necessary that the actual flow of stock usage follows this pattern for this method to be applied.

Assume the following:

Purchases

16.1.02	100	units @	R2	200
25.1.02	100	units @	R3	300
	200	units		R500

Usage

14.1.02	50	units
17.1.02	20	units
30.1.02	40	units
	110	units

Stock 1.1.02 was 100 units @ R1   R100

In other words at 31.1.02 stock on hand amounted to 190 units

i.e. Stock at 1.1.02	100	
Purchased	200	
	300	
Used	110	
	190	units

Applying FIFO the assumption made is that the stock on hand at 31.1.02 is made up of

100 units purchased on 25.1.02	@ R3	300
and 90 units purchased on 16.1.02	@ R2	180
		R480

The cost of sales for the month of January 02 would be:

Stock 1.1.02	100
Purchases	500
	600
Stock 31.1.02	480
Cost of sales	R120

Alternatively this could be calculated as follows:

Usage	14.1.02	50 units @ R1		50
Usage	17.1.02	20 units @ R1		20
Usage	30.1.02	30 units @ R1	30	
	and	10 units @ R2	20	
		40 units		50
Cost of sales				R120

The valuation of stock on a FIFO basis tends to result in a balance sheet figure which is closely related to the current value but a cost of sales figure which is understated, hence overstating profits.

LIFO

Another method which is sometimes used is the one referred to as Last In–First Out (LIFO). This method of valuation is based on the assumption that the most recently acquired items of stock on hand are used first. The items remaining in stock are therefore the items purchased first. As with FIFO it is not necessary that the actual flow of stock items follows this pattern for LIFO to be applied. If this were the case, the implications for an egg wholesaler which applied LIFO could be offensive, if not disastrous.

In order to apply LIFO to the information earlier in this chapter we need to establish how the level of stock has fluctuated. This could be done as follows:

					R
Stock 1.1.02	100	units @ R1			100
Usage 14.1.02	50	units @ R1			50
Balance	50	units @ R1			50
Purchases 16.1.02	100	units @ R2			200
Balance	50	units @ R1	50		
	100	units @ R2	200		
	150				250
Usage 17.1.02	20	units @ R2			40
Balance	50	units @ R1	50		
	80	units @ R2	160		
	130				210
Purchases 25.1.02	100	units @ R3			300
Balance	50	units @ R1	50		
	80	units @ R2	160		
	100	units @ R3	300		
	230				510
Usage 30.1.02	40	units @ R3			120
Stock 31.1.02	50	units @ R1	50		
	80	units @ R2	160		
	60	units @ R3	180		
	190				390

The cost of sales for the month of January 02 would be:

Stock 1.1.02	100
Purchases	500
	600
Stock 31.1.02	390
Cost of sales	R210

Alernatively this could be calculated as follows:

Usage 14.1.02	50 units @ R1	50
Usage 17.1.02	20 units @ R2	40
Usage 30.1.02	40 units @ R3	120
Cost of sales		R210

This last calculation illustrates the theoretical application of LIFO. However, in practice LIFO is generally applied by reference to the opening and closing stock levels without taking into account the fluctuations of stock levels within the period as indicated by the stock records. If this were applied the calculation would be:

Stock 31.1.02 consists of	
100 units @ R1	100
90 units @ R2	180
	R280

The cost of sales calculation would be

Stock 1.1.02	100
Purchases	500
	600
Stock 31.1.02	280
Cost of sales	R320

Alternatively this could be calculated as follows:

Usage during the period based on last items purchased, being used first	
Total usage 110 units	
i.e. 100 units @ R3	300
10 units @ R2	20
Cost of sales	R320

A comparison of the methods shows how vastly differing figures can result from the same transactions.

	FIFO	LIFO Theoretical Application	LIFO Practical Application
Cost of sales	120	210	320
Stock 31.1.02	480	390	280

Comparing the above it can be seen that whichever of the LIFO applications is used, using LIFO in times of rising prices will result in a higher cost of sales figure and a lower stock figure, than will arise from the use of FIFO.

LIFO would (if allowed as a basis for calculating the liability for taxation) improve cash flow. Using LIFO profits and taxation are deferred to later periods. This is because LIFO results in lower taxable income consequent upon a higher charge for cost of sales.

However, the disadvantages are that stock tends to be valued below its real value during times of rising prices and the associated administrative cost may be high.

An over-riding consideration in stock valuation is that whichever method is used to calculate the cost of stock on hand a comparison is made to the net realisable value of the stock. This ensures that it is not shown in the balance sheet at a value greater than its selling price. Although during a time of decreasing prices LIFO may result in a lower cost of sales than FIFO this may, to some extent, be obviated by the comparison to net realisable value.

WEIGHTED AVERAGE

The weighted average method of stock valuation involves averaging the cost of the stock, based on the differing purchase prices and the relative quantities purchased at these prices. Applying this to the information used earlier in this chapter the valuation is as follows:

		R
Stock 1.1.02	100 units @ R1	100
Usage 14.1.02	50 units @ R1	50
Balance	50 units @ R1	50
Purchase 16.1.02	100 units @ R2	200
Balance 150 units @ R1,67 [R250 ÷ 150]		250
Usage 17.1.02	20 units @ R1,67	33
Balance	130 units @ R1,67	217
Purchases 25.1.02	100 units @ R3	300
Balance 230 units @ R2,25 [R517 ÷ 230]		517
Usage 30.1.02	40 units @ R2,25	90
Stock 31.1.02	190 units @ R2,25	427

The cost of sales for the month of January 02 would be:

Stock 1.1.02	100
Purchases	500
	600
Stock 31.1.02	427
Cost of sales	R173

From a comparison with FIFO and LIFO it can be seen that the weighted average method smooths the effect of changing prices, by arriving at a stock valuation and cost of sales somewhere between those arrived at by the FIFO and LIFO methods.

The major disadvantage of the weighted average method is the volume of computations that must be performed. Computerisation could ease this problem.

OTHER METHODS

There are several other methods. One frequently encountered is the valuation of stock at standard costs. This is dealt with in the chapter on Standard Costing.

Other methods include Next-In-First-Out (NIFO), net realisable value, and current cost.

WORK IN PROGRESS

The principles discussed above apply equally to the valuation of work in progress.

Work in progress is discussed further in the chapters dealing with job, process and contract costing.

QUESTIONS

5.1 In each of the following cases indicate whether the fact/s stated are true or false:

(a) The proper valuation of stock can often be vital as a result of the significance which it may have on the result reported.

(b) The policy adopted for stock valuation is irrelevant as its value will not vary with the use of different policies.

(c) Using LIFO to value stock will result in a more accurate income statement but an under-stated balance sheet figure during periods of rising prices.

(d) A comparison of the figure derived for stock to net realisable value should always be made, irrespective of how the value was derived.

(e) The method used to value stock must always mirror the actual physical flow of the stock.

5.2 From the following information value the stock at the end of March using FIFO and LIFO.

What is the cost of sales for the period using each of the methods and assuming there was no stock on hand at the beginning of the period.

QUANTITY

Date	Purchased	Used	Unit cost
5.01	50 000		5,00
18.01		30 000	
29.01	65 000		5,10
3.02	4 000		5,05
21.02		53 000	
27.02		5 000	
6.03	14 500		5,25
8.03		7 500	
16.03	45 000		5,80
23.03		31 000	
29.03		3 500	

6 Cost Classification and Absorption

It is imperative to know the cost of production or the cost of goods or services provided, irrespective of the type of business and the sophistication of management.

The knowledge of the cost of a product has two major uses. It is an important factor in the pricing of the product and in the control of costs.

Without knowing the cost of production, pricing may be haphazard. While it may be true that market forces play an important role in pricing a product, so, too, does the cost of that product.

Furthermore control of costs is made very difficult if not impossible without a thorough knowledge and understanding of the relevant costs. In other words, before a product can be costed an understanding of the nature and behaviour of costs is required. The classification of costs assists in this understanding.

COST CLASSIFICATION

Costs may be classified in any way that management finds useful. It is often more convenient to group costs and deal with them in a certain manner rather than taking a decision about each particular cost.

Any group may be classified in an infinitesmal number of ways. People may be classified as tall or short, fat or thin, pretty or ugly, or by nationality, or race, or religion, etc. Costs may also be classified in different ways. The method of classification chosen will depend on the purpose for which the classification is being undertaken.

In this chapter the objective is to determine a carrying value for a product, thus the cost classification chosen will be aimed at facilitating this objective.

Classifications are not mutually exclusive. Because a cost is placed into a particular classification does not preclude it from being placed into another classification at the same time. Consider a person who is tall, thin, fair, Austrian. He has been classified in four ways, which may be useful to someone.

The most common classifications used for product costing are:

1. Type of expenditure
2. Function
3. Behaviour
4. Traceability

Type of Expenditure

This classification intuitively encompasses such familiar categories as materials, labour and other expenses. Take a dressmaker who has the following expenses for a particular week:

Cloth used	R100
Assistant's wages	R 50
Rent	R200
Thread used	R 10
Salesman's salary	R 40
Telephone	R 20

These expenses may be classified in terms of their type as follows:

	Materials	Labour	Other Expenses
Cloth	100		
Assistant		50	
Rent			200
Thread	10		
Salesman		40	
Telephone			20
	110	90	220

Total R420

The dressmaker now knows that in that week he spent R110 on materials, R90 on labour and incurred other expenditure of R220. This information is useful to the dressmaker but it is not sufficient to cost his products as he is likely to have made several dresses of different styles, sizes and quality. Thus further classifications are required.

It is customary for materials to include all costs of getting the materials to the factory, labour to include all levies and benefits paid on behalf of employees, and expenses to include non-cash expenditure such as depreciation.

If these expense categories are considered too broad, management may expand them, e.g. labour may be split into skilled and unskilled. If a particular type of expenditure is considered important to the business it may be categorised separately. The over-riding factor to remember in determining classifications is that they must be useful to the particular circumstances.

Function

The usual functional classifications are manufacturing, administration and selling. Other common categories are financial expenses, research and development.

Applying these categories to the example of the dressmaker:

	Manu-facture	Adminis-tration	Selling	
Cloth	100			
Assistant's wages	50			
Rent	200			
Thread	10			
Saleman's salary			40	
Telephone		20		
	360	20	40	R420

The dressmaker now has a better understanding of what went into the manufacture of the products. Clearly the combination of this classificaiton with the type of expenditure is even more beneficial, e.g. manufacturing costs are made up of:

materials	R110
labour	50
other expenses	200
	R360

Note that in this case the rental charge of R200 has been classified as a manufacturing expense. In most factories the various departments all attract certain common costs such as rent, which may be apportioned to them.

At this stage it may still not be possible to cost the product as the R360 which has been determined may be related to the manufacturing cost of several differing lines of dresses.

Behaviour

Costs behave differently in relation to output: they can be fixed or variable.

Fixed costs are those costs that do not change with changes in the level of output (Fig. 6.1 (a)).

Variable costs are those costs that change proportionately with changes in the level of output (Fig. 6.1 (b)).

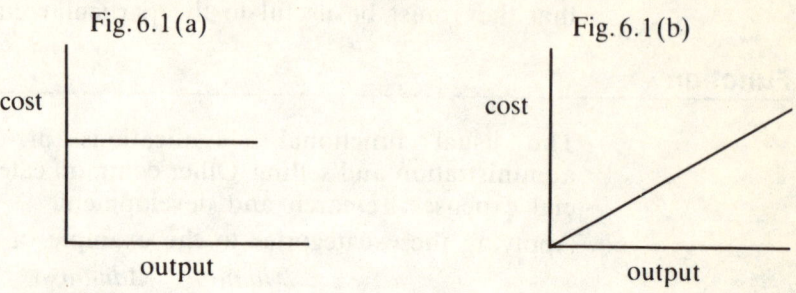

From Fig. 6.1 (a) it can be seen that total fixed cost remains the same irrespective of output. Examples of fixed costs may be rent, management salaries and depreciation.

It is vital to be aware that fixed costs are only fixed over a relevant range. For example, the rent may remain constant when a factory produces 100 or 110 units a day. However, if the factory produced no units it is possible that operations may be discontinued and no rent would be incurred if the lease agreement could be terminated. Conversely, if the factory reaches full capacity at 120 units, and 150 units are to be produced then additional premises may have to be found and additional rent incurred.

While all costs are variable over a sufficiently long period of time and a sufficiently wide range, costs may be classified as fixed or variable within the constraint of the relevant range of activity.

A further factor is that some costs are step-variable (Fig. 6.2 (a)) and others are semi-variable (Fig. 6.2 (b)).

Step-variable costs are those that increase intermittently with relatively small increases in the level of output. It is usually acceptable to treat them as variable bearing in mind the relevant range.

Semi-variable costs are those that have a fixed portion and a variable portion, e.g. a salesman paid on a salary and commission basis. The salary may be regarded as fixed but the commission varies with output. It is best to deal with the fixed and variable elements of semi-variable costs separately.

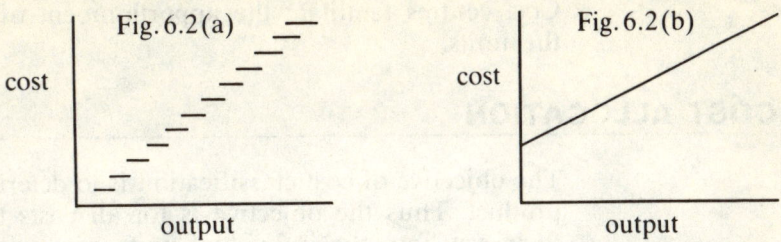

With most costs it is not possible to lay down a hard and fast rule as to whether they are fixed or variable; it depends on the circumstances of each particular case. Applying this to the costs incurred in the example of the dressmaker,

Materials — variable

Assistant's wages — productive wages are usually treated as variable. But remember that it is not always easy to hire and fire staff at will.

Rent — usually fixed.

Salesman's salary — fixed (assuming no commission in this case).

Telephone — usually treated as variable although probably more accurately described as semi-variable, as there is a fixed portion in the telephone rental.

Traceability

Costs may either be closely related to a unit of production or they may be related to several units of production. If a cost is closely related to a unit or is easily traceable to that unit it is said to be a direct cost; if not it is an indirect cost.

Indirect costs may however be easily traceable to something other than the unit produced. For example, they may be easily related to a machine, or a department in a factory, or to the operation carried out under a particular foreman, which are known as cost centres.

A cost centre is any part of the business to which costs may be charged.

Costs which are easily traced to particular units are direct costs in relation to those units. Other costs which are not so traceable are indirect to the cost units. Costs which are easily traced to a particular cost centre are direct costs in relation to those cost centres. Other costs which are not so traceable are indirect to the cost centre.

Costs that are indirect in relation to cost units are also known as overheads.

Cost centres facilitate the apportionment of indirect costs to the units.

COST ALLOCATION

The objective of cost classification is to determine the cost of a product. Thus the objective is for all costs to ultimately find their way into the individual units of production.

But do all costs mean every cost incurred by the business? No. It is only manufacturing costs that should be allocated to the product. Administrative and selling costs are dealt with in the income statement.

The relevance of fixed and variable cost classification will become more evident when the allocation of the overheads to the products is examined.

Refer to Fig. 6.3.

Costs which are indirect in relation to cost centres are allocated to the cost centres on some equitable common-sense basis, examples are:

rent—on the basis of floor space;
factory manager's salary—on the basis of time spent in each department.

The costs allocated to service departments are then also allocated to the productive departments in a similar manner.

The problem then is how to allocate the costs allocated to the productive departments, to the individual units produced?

The basis of allocating overheads to the units should be related to the factor that causes the overheads to be incurred or that bears a close relationship to the overheads being incurred.

Some common examples of bases of allocation are:

1. Labour hour rate or a machine hour rate—these are both related to time and would be used in a situation where overheads are incurred because of the passage of time. The labour hour rate would normally be used in a labour intensive factory and the machine hour rate in a machine intensive factory.

2. Percentage of direct wages—overheads are related to a grade of labour and therefore the higher grades of labour will incur a greater labour charge and consequently a greater portion of overhead costs.

3. Rate per unit—is used where products are similar and therefore it is equitable that they bear an equal portion of overhead costs.

Fig. 6.3 illustrates the route followed in allocating costs to the individual units.

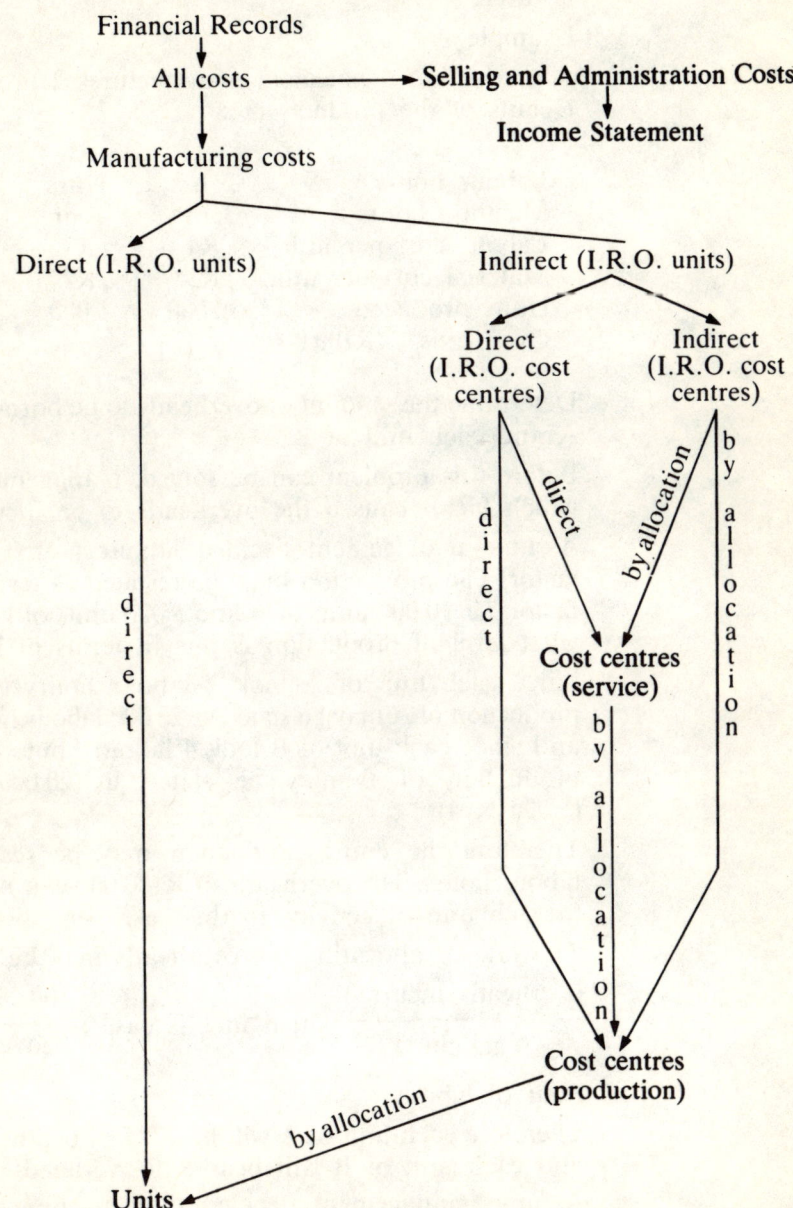

Overheads may be allocated in any way which bears a causal relationship to their being incurred. As long as management considers there to be a relationship between the incurrence of the overheads and the factor chosen, then that factor may be used.

Example:

A production department manufactures 2 products, A and B. Details of the products are:

	A	B
Labour hours	2 hrs	4 hrs
Machine hours	3 hrs	1 hr
Labour cost per unit	R4	R7
Material cost per unit	R2	R2
Units produced	10 000	5 000
Overheads R100 000		

Determine the amount of overheads to be borne by each unit of A and each unit of B.

Before this problem can be solved, management must decide which factor caused the overheads to be incurred.

Assume management decided labour hours was the causal factor. The production must be restated in terms of the causal factor, i.e. 10 000 units of A and 5 000 units of B were produced, what level of production is this in terms of labour hours?

Since each unit of A took 2 labour hours to complete, the production of A may be stated as 20 000 labour hours (10 000 × 2) and since each unit of B took 4 labour hours to complete, the production of B may be stated as 20 000 labour hours (5 000 × 4).

Therefore the entire production may be restated as 40 000 labour hours. The overheads of R100 000 can now be allocated to each unit of activity, in this case per labour hour.

The rate of allocating the overheads may be expressed as

$$\frac{\text{overheads incurred}}{\text{activity}} \text{ which in this case is } \frac{100\,000}{40\,000} \text{ or R2,50 per}$$

hour of labour.

Therefore each unit of A will bear R5 of overheads (2 × R2,50) and each unit of B will bear R10 overheads (4 × R2,50).

Assume management decided that machine hours was the causal factor.

The activity expressed in terms of machine hours would be 35 000 hours [(10 000 × 3) + (5 000 × 1)]. Therefore the overheads of R100 000 would be allocated at a rate of

$$\frac{100\,000}{35\,000} = R2,85 \text{ per machine hour.}$$

Therefore each unit of A will bear R8,55 and each unit of B will bear R2,85.

Note how these figures differ from those calculated under the labour hour rate. This emphasises the importance of selecting the correct causal factor on which to base the allocation of overheads. From the information given the overheads per unit to be allocated to each of the products may be calculated on a:

	A	B
—Labour cost basis (total labour cost R75 000)	[40/75 × 100 000 ÷ 10 000] R5,33/unit	[35/75 × 100 000 ÷ 5 000] R9,33/unit
—Material cost basis (total material cost R30 000)	[20/30 × 100 000 ÷ 10 000] R6,67/unit	[10/30 × 100 000 ÷ 5 000] R6,67/unit
—Unit basis (total units produced 15 000 units)	[10/15 × 100 000 ÷ 10 000] R6,67/unit	[5/15 × 100 000 ÷ 5 000] R6,67/unit

TOTAL COST

With the classifications considered in this chapter it is now possible to see how the costs in a business relate to each other.

DIRECT MATERIAL
+ DIRECT LABOUR
+ INDIRECT MANUFACTURING COST
   (or manufacturing overheads)
_____

= MANUFACTURING COST
+ ADMINISTRATION COST
+ SELLING & DISTRIBUTION COST
_____

= TOTAL COST
_____

The manufacturing cost section may be broken up into two other useful segments.

Direct material and direct labour together form what is known as PRIME COST. This may be intuitively derived, as any object manufactured consists primarily of materials and labour.

Direct labour and manufacturing overheads together are termed CONVERSION COST. This may also be intuitively derived, as labour and overheads are applied to the materials to convert them into manfactured goods.

OVERHEAD ABSORPTION RATE

Until now the classification of costs has been examined so that products may be costed. Management, however, needs to cost its products in advance.

To allocate costs accurately to production one needs the actual production and actual cost information. It is not feasible to wait until the end of the year when the year's activity is known and the year's overheads are known, to do this. Management must therefore estimate the allocation rate, based on their expectations, to cost products and derive other pertinent information during the year.

Earlier the allocation rate (also known as the absorption rate) for overheads was expressed as:

Overheads
  activity

To determine the absorption rate management must estimate the expected activity level and also estimate the expected overheads, both fixed and variable. The overheads absorption rates may be expressed as:

$$\frac{\text{estimated fixed overhead}}{\text{estimated activity}} = \text{fixed overhead absorption rate}$$

and

$$\frac{\text{estimated variable overhead}}{\text{estimated activity}} = \text{variable overhead absorption rate.}$$

These two rates added together give a total overhead absorption rate. This figure is sometimes used so that only one instead of two amounts have to be added to the prime cost to determine the cost of a product. However, even if the two are added together and one rate is used it cannot be over-emphasised that conceptually and practically there are two rates which, as shall be seen later, have different characteristics.

While the fixed overhead absorption rate is set by estimating expenditure and activity, the variable overhead absorption rate is set by estimating the rate. The very nature of variable costs causes this to arise. Remember variable costs are costs which vary with activity. It is impossible to estimate the variable costs unless the activity and the rate are estimated first.

At the end of the year if the overheads absorbed are compared with the overheads incurred there is likely to be a difference. The difference may arise in the case of fixed overheads because management incorrectly estimated either the amount of the overheads or the activity. In the case of variable overheads the difference may arise due to an incorrect estimate of the rate. If more overheads were absorbed than incurred, this is referred to as an overabsorption and if less overheads were absorbed than incurred, this is referred to as an underabsorption. Over- and underabsorption of overheads may be illustrated graphically.

Fixed Overhead Absorption

Fig. 6.4

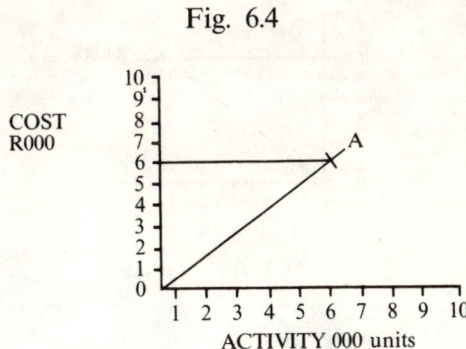

If management estimated fixed overheads to be R6 000 and the activity level to be 6 000 units, then the absorption rate will be R1 per unit. The absorption is represented by the line OA; thus if 1 000 units are produced R1 000 will be absorbed, if 1 100 units are produced, R1 100 will be absorbed, etc.

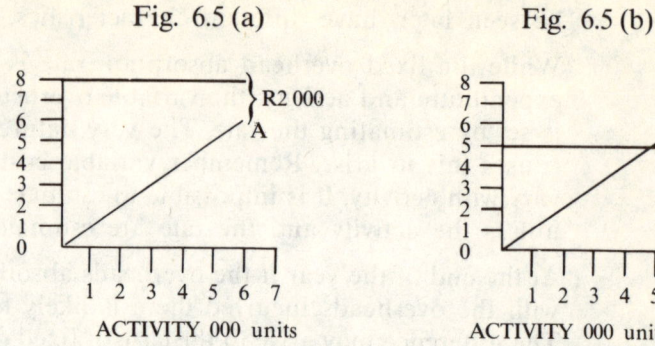

Fig. 6.5 (a)   Fig. 6.5 (b)

ACTIVITY 000 units   ACTIVITY 000 units

In Figs. 6.5 (a) and (b) the absorption line is the same as in Fig. 6.4 as management expected 6 000 units to be produced and overheads of R6 000 to be incurred. If in fact 6 000 units were produced but R8 000 was incurred then there will be an underabsorption of R2 000 [R8 000 − (6 000 × R1)]. This is represented in Fig. 6.5 (a).

Figure 6.5 (b) represents the overabsorption that occurs where estimates are as in Fig. 6.4 but in fact overheads of only R5 000 are incurred.

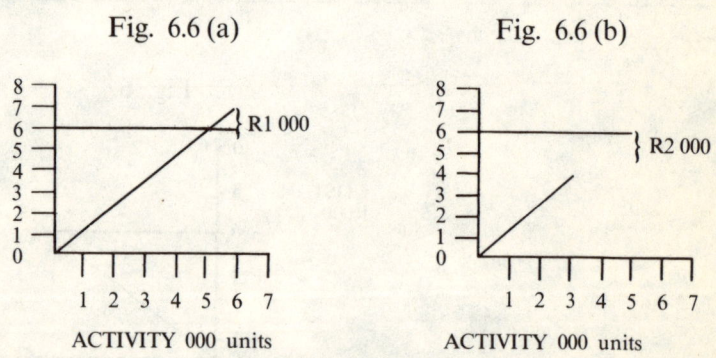

Fig. 6.6 (a)   Fig. 6.6 (b)

ACTIVITY 000 units   ACTIVITY 000 units

Figures 6.6 (a) and (b) represent the situation where the overheads were correctly estimated but the activity level was not. As can be seen from Fig. 6.6 (a): while only R6 000 of overheads were incurred, each unit produced absorbed R1 even though more than 6 000 units were produced resulting in an over-absorption of R1 000 [R6 000 − (7 000 × R1)]. While in the case of Fig. 6.6 (b) although only 4 000 units were produced, absorbing overhead of R4 000, the costs incurred still amounted to R6 000, resulting in an underabsorption of R2 000 [R6 000 − (4 000 × R1)].

Of course over- and underabsorption may be caused by a combination of incorrect estimates, i.e. if both the activity level and the amount of overheads are incorrectly estimated.

Variable Overhead Absorption

Fig. 6.7

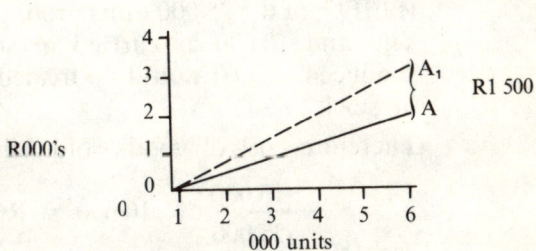

If variable overheads are estimated to be 50c per unit and 6 000 units are produced then the line OA represents the absorption line. However, if the variable overheads are incurred at a rate of 75c per unit then the line OA_1 represents the variable overheads spent at a level of 6 000 units. The gap between the lines at the actual activity level represents the over- or underabsorption. In this case an underabsorption of R1 500 [R6 000 × (75c − 50c)].

Arithmetically the figure would be calculated by applying the following logic:

Amount spent	R4 500
Amount expected to be spent and consequently charged to (absorbed by) production	
50c a unit × 6 000 units	3 000
Therefore underabsorbed	R1 500

How are the resultant over- or underabsorptions, if any, treated in costing the products? This depends on the reason for the variation. If the cause was a one-off event, management may be content to write the over- or underabsorption off in the income statement and not tamper with the cost of production, e.g. a work stoppage due to a fire in the factory.

The alternative is to adjust the cost of goods manufactured. Depending on whether these goods are still in stock or have been sold, this entails adjusting either the stock records or the costs of sales.

If the factory manufactures only 1 type of product, and there were 5 000 units in opening stock, 25 000 were produced during the year, 20 000 were sold and 10 000 were on hand at the end of the year and overheads were underabsorbed by R10 000. The R10 000 must be taken to the cost of production, i.e. added to the cost of the 25 000 units produced.

But the exact amount to be taken to cost of goods sold and to closing stock depends on the basis of stock valuation.

If FIFO; of the 25 000 units produced, 15 000 would be treated as sold and 10 000 as carried in stock. If LIFO; of the 25 000 produced, 20 000 would be treated as sold and 5 000 as carried in stock.

Therefore cost of goods sold will be increased by:

$$\frac{15\,000}{25\,000} \times 10\,000 = R6\,000 \text{ under FIFO and by}$$

$$\frac{20\,000}{25\,000} \times 10\,000 = R8\,000 \text{ under LIFO}$$

And closing stock will be increased by:

$$\frac{10\,000}{25\,000} \times 10\,000 = R4\,000 \text{ under FIFO and by}$$

$$\frac{5\,000}{25\,000} \times 10\,000 = R2\,000 \text{ under LIFO}$$

More importantly, from a decision-making point of view management must carefully consider this change and whether it can be controlled or not. If it is permanent then the cost of production for the next period must be adjusted to take this into account.

QUESTIONS

6.1 What is a cost centre? Why is a cost centre useful in costing a product?

6.2 For each of the following costs indicate whether they are likely to be fixed or variable and direct or indirect.
1. Raw materials
2. Foreman's salary
3. Factory labour
4. Factory rent

5. Delivery expenses
6. Accounting service
7. Managing director's salary
8. Depreciation of machinery
9. Depreciation of office furniture
10. Night watchman's wages.

6.3 A factory manufactures 2 products A & B. Details for a month are:

	A	B
Units produced	1 000	1 200
Materials	R10	R20
Labour hours	5	3
Machine hours	9	12
Selling price	R50	R75

Overheads for the month amounted to R100 000.

Required

Allocate the overhead to the products on as many different bases as the data permit. Explain why each of the bases may be used.

7 Product Costing

As mentioned in Chapter 6, the cost of a product is one of the most important figures needed by management.

The cost of a product may be determined either by job costing or by process costing. The method chosen depends on the nature of the product being costed. Where the material cost or the labour cost is easily traced to the cost unit then job costing is used. Examples include manufactured furniture, printing and construction.

Where the individual cost components are not easily traced to the units produced then process costing is used; most chemical processes fall into this category.

To illustrate further: a furniture manufacturer uses a piece of wood, some nails and glue, applies some labour and produces a table. The piece of wood used is easily traced to the table produced. Contrast this with a petrol refinery where crude oil is processed. A litre of crude oil is not traceable to a specific litre of refined petrol at the other end. In the case of the petrol refinery process costing would be used.

A feature of job costing is that although many similar items may be produced they don't all necessarily pass through the identical process. Again contrast the furniture manufacturer and the petrol refinery. The furniture manufacturer makes cupboards. He may make many cupboards, but each one is not necessarily made in the same way as the others. Whereas in the case of the petrol refinery, each litre of oil is identically processed.

A method of costing similar to job costing is batch costing. Batch costing is the same as job costing except that more than one item at a time is made. The characteristics remain the same in that the costs are identifiable to the individual units, e.g., the furniture manufacturer may make not one table but 10 or 100 tables at a time. At some stage batch costing becomes process costing. The distinction between them is very fine.

JOB COSTING

In job costing each job will normally have a separate record usually called a job card. The entries to the job card are taken from a variety of documents such as the material requisition notes in respect of the materials, the work tickets or time cards in respect of labour, and the overheads applied on the predetermined absorption basis discussed in the previous chapter.

An example of a job card familiar to most readers is the motor repair bill. It is a job card, except that the overhead absorption is not separately stated, it is normally included in the labour charge as are overheads and profit.

At any point the total of the job cards should equal the work-in-progress account in the ledger in the same way that the total of each individual ledger account equals the debtor's control account in the nominal ledger. When the job is finished the job card is taken out of the file for incompleted jobs and put in the file for completed jobs and a journal entry is passed in the general ledger transferring the work-in-progress account to the finished goods account. In this way not only is the book-keeping recorded but there is also the control aspect whereby the job cards can be agreed to the work-in-progress account, and the finished goods to the finished goods account in the nominal ledger.

Illustrative Example

A company is engaged in the manufacture of furniture. During the week in question, 3 jobs were worked on. There were no opening stocks. During the week

100 metres of wood at R10 per metre were purchased —	R1 000
80 hours of direct labour at R5 per hour were worked and paid for —	R 400
Overheads incurred and paid —	R 200

Material issued to jobs was:

Job no 1	30 metres
Job no 2	20 metres
Job no 3	40 metres

Direct labour hours worked on the jobs:

Job no 1	20 hours
Job no 2	15 hours
Job no 3	45 hours

Overheads are applied at R2 per direct labour hour.

At the end of the week Job no 1 had been completed and sold.
Job no 2 had been completed but was not yet sold.
Job no 3 was incomplete.

The relevant entries and accounts to record the above would be:

1. Entries recording the acquisition of goods and services:

	Debit	Credit
Material stock	1 000	
Accounts payable		1 000
Purchase of 100 metres of wood		
Labour control	400	
Cash		400
80 hours of labour paid		
Overhead control	200	
Accounts payable		200
Various overheads paid for		

2. Entries recording the application of goods and services to jobs:

	Debit	Credit
Work in progress	900	
Material stock		900
Issue of wood to jobs as follows:		
Job no 1: 30 metres	R300	
Job no 2: 20 metres	200	
Job no 3: 40 metres	400	
	R900	

	Debit	Credit
Work in progress	400	
Labour control		400
Application of labour to jobs:		
Job no 1: 20 hours	100	
Job no 2: 15 hours	75	
Job no 3: 45 hours	225	
	R400	

	Debit	Credit
Work in progress	160	
Overhead control		160
Allocation of overheads to jobs:		
Job no 1: 20 hours	40	
Job no 2: 15 hours	30	
Job no 3: 45 hours	90	
	R160	

3. Entry recording the transfer of finished goods:

Finished goods stock	745	
Work in progress		745
Jobs completed transferred to		
finished goods stock		
Job no 1	440	
Job no 2	305	
	R745	

4. Entry recording the removal of goods sold from stock:

Cost of sales	440	
Finished goods stock		440
Job no 1 sold		

JOB CARDS

Job 1

Material	
30 metres @ R10/metre	300
Labour	
20 hours @ R5/hour	100
Overheads	
20 hours @ R2/hour	40
Total cost to date	440

Comments:
Goods completed
Goods sold

Job 2

Material	
20 metres @ R10/metre	200
Labour	
15 hours @ R5/hour	75
Overheads	
15 hours @ R2/hour	30
Total cost to date	305

Comments:
Goods completed

Job 3

Material

   40 metres @ R10/metre   400

Labour

   45 hours @ R5/hour   225

Overheads

   45 hours @ R2/hour   90

Total cost to date   715

Comments:

   Incomplete

LEDGER ACCOUNTS

Material Stock

Accounts Payable	1 000	Work in Progress	900
		Balance	100
	R1 000		R1 000
Balance	100		

Labour Control

Cash	400	Work in Progress	400

Overhead Control

Accounts Payable	200	Work in Progress	160
		Balance	40
	R200		R200
Balance	40		

Work in Progress

Material	900	Finished Goods	745
Labour	400	Balance	715
Overheads	160		
	R1 460		R1 460
Balance	715		

Finished Goods

Work in Progress	745	Cost of Sales	440
		Balance	305
	R745		R745
Balance	305		

Cost of Sales

Finished Goods	440	Trading Account	440

Note that job card no 1 will be filed as the goods have been sold.

Job card no 2 is in agreement with the finished goods account in the ledger and should be represented by finished goods in the store.

Job card no 3 is in agreement with the Work in Progress (WIP) account in the ledger and should be represented by incompleted goods on the factory floor.

The balance on the material stock account should be represented by wood in the storeroom. The balance on the overhead control account represents an underabsorption of overheads and should be dealt with as discussed in Chapter 6.

Spoilage

The terms spoilage, wastage, scrap and defective units are used interchangeably, there are minor differences but they may be treated as the same. Spoilage may be split into two broad categories, normal and abnormal.

Normal spoilage is expected to arise under efficient operating conditions. Examples may be off-cuts in a furniture factory or evaporation in the case of a petrol refinery. These are expected, they form part of the cost of the job and are charged to the product.

Abnormal spoilage is not expected to arise under efficient operating conditions. For example, if a petrol truck crashes and the petrol spills out, or a plank is too long and is cracked, these are not expected and cannot be charged to the particular job as expected spoilage. Instead the cost of abnormal spoilage is written off. It cannot be taken to the cost of the product nor can it be inventoried; it is written off in the income statement, and is regarded as a cost of inefficiency.

For example: A job consists of making 15 gadgets at a cost of R2 each. On completion it is found that 5 gadgets are spoilt and must be scrapped. How is the spoilage treated? The entry, which would have been put through as the job was carried out is, debit to work in progress of R30 [15 × 2] and credits to material control, labour control and overhead control accounts of a total of R30. If the spoilage were abnormal, the R10 [5 × 2] would be written off to the income statement. If the spoilage is normal, then no entry is passed as the work in progress will now represent only 10 units and not 15 units and thus the expected cost per unit, taking into account normal spoilage, is R3. This is the treatment adopted most frequently in practice. There is a theoretically more satisfactory method of dealing with normal spoilage. This is to charge it to the overhead control account as the overhead absorption rate would have made allowance for this normal spoilage so that the absorption rate would consequently have been higher.

If the spoilage has a resale value, the cost of scrap will be credited to the work-in-progress account, and will not form part of the cost of the finished goods. The debit will go to a scrap stock account. When it is sold it will be charged to a sale of scrap account. A point to note about normal spoilage is that although it is expected under efficient operating conditions, it could often be eliminated. However, the cost of eliminating all spoilage may be greater than the savings generated. In the case of the oil refinery, although methods to eliminate evaporation may be available, the cost of this would undoubtedly be prohibitive, taking into account the value of the benefit. It is far better to expect and be aware of a certain amount of spoilage.

Example

Produced 20 units @ R3
5 spoilt
11 sold for R5
Other expenses R7

(a) If spoilage is treated as normal spoilage

Sales [11 × 5]		R55
Cost of sales		
Manufacturing cost [15 × 4]*	60	
Closing stock [4 × 4]	16	
		44
		11
Other expenses		7
Net profit		4

* Cost of R60 [20 × 3] allocated to 15 good units of production.

(b) If spoilage is treated as abnormal spoilage

Sales [11 × 5]		R55
Cost of sales		
Manufacturing cost [15 × 3]	45	
Stock [4 × 3]	12	
		33
		22
Other expenses	7	
Abnormal spoilage [5 × 3]	15	
		22
		NIL

Note:

The difference of R4 between (a) and (b) is because (a) treated the spoilage as normal. Consequently it had a higher stock value and therefore a higher profit would be recorded as the cost of spoilage of R1 per unit has been carried forward to the next period. Case (b) has written off all spoilage as abnormal in the current period.

PROCESS COSTING

In job costing the individual cost components can be traced to each particular product. Process costing is a method of averaging the product cost where the cost of each individual unit cannot be traced. Thus it is an accumulation of all the costs involved in making all the units and averaging the total costs over the total output.

Given that at the end of any period there will usually be production in progress, which may contain differing relative levels of input of the various cost components, a problem exists in apportioning the cost incurred between finished goods and work in progress.

This may be dealt with by expressing the output, both complete and in progress, in terms of completed production, sometimes referred to as equivalent units of production.

Assume that at the end of the period there are 1 000 units which are 60% finished. We can say we have produced the same as 600 units, that is 60% of 1 000, or in other words, there are 600 equivalent units of production in progress.

In practice a variety of methods are used, but they generally rely on the application of the concept of equivalent units.

For example 200 units are started, 140 are completed, the other 60 units are one third complete at the end of a period. In this particular process all materials are added at the beginning of the process. The costs incurred during the period are materials R600 and labour R320.

Valuation of finished goods and work in progress

	Materials	Labour
Started and completed 140	140	140
Closing work in progress 60	60	20
Equivalent units	200	160
Costs to be accounted for	R600	R320 = R920
Costs per equivalent unit	R3	R2 = R5

Cost of goods transferred to finished goods stock (140 units)
$$140 \times 5 = R700$$

Cost of work in progress (60 units)

Material (60 × 3)	180	
Labour (20 × 2)	40	220
Costs accounted for		R920

Note that in calculating the equivalent units of labour for the work in progress, in order to cost 60 units which are one third complete, we use 20 equivalent units $(60 \times \frac{1}{3})$ of production.

In dealing with process costing problems, it is useful to follow the steps suggested by Horngren and Foster.*

Step 1   Trace the physical flow of the goods, i.e. how many units went into production, and where did they go, finished goods, work in progress, spoilt or transferred out.

Step 2   Convert into equivalent units.

Step 3   Establish the total cost to account for, that is add up all the costs, viz. materials, labour, overheads and cost of opening stock.

Step 4   Calculate the cost per equivalent unit.

Step 5   Account for the costs related to finished goods and work in progress on the basis of equivalent units calculated in Step 4.

The total costs accounted for in Step 5 should equal the costs of input, that is the total of the costs listed in Step 3.

* Horngren, C. and Foster, G.—Cost accounting: A managerial emphasis.

The costs of inputs may include labour, overheads and materials added, as well as the cost of goods from a previous stage in the production process. The costs of those partially finished goods from a previous process are called transferred-in costs. Those goods are finished as regards the previous process and are brought in merely as another raw material and may be treated as such in the current process. The convenient way to view this is to regard the transferred in goods simply as another raw material, bought from an outside supplier.

Process costing is a technique for establishing the cost of output. As with other techniques the valuation basis depends on the valuation policy adopted by the business. (As discussed in Chapter 5, this may be one of a number of bases.) The following example illustrates the application of both FIFO and weighted average. Under the FIFO method of valuing stock, the units produced in each period are separately identified. Using FIFO the costs of goods started and completed will differ from the cost of opening stock completed.

The weighted average method does not account for the period in which production was started. The whole of the work in progress at the beginning of the period is included in the equivalent units calculation. The previous period costs are added to the costs incurred during the current period and applied to all equivalent units, resulting in an average cost.

In FIFO equivalent units are added only to the portion which is completed in the current period. The cost of the opening work in progress does not form part of the calculation of the current period's cost per equivalent unit.

Illustrative Example

A company manufactures ARPS, details for the period are:

Opening WIP	100 kg	60% complete
Materials added	500 kg	
Finished goods	400 kg	
Closing WIP	200 kg	70% complete

Materials are added at the beginning of the process.
The cost of opening WIP was—
    Materials R190, Labour R50.
Costs during the period were—
    Materials R1 000, Labour R480.

Applying FIFO

	Units	Materials	Labour
Opening WIP	100	—	40
Started and completed	300	300	300
Closing WIP	200	200	140
Equivalent units		500	480
Costs for the period		1 000	480
Cost per equivalent unit		R2	R1

Costs to be accounted for:

WIP bfwd	240
Materials	1 000
Labour	480
	R1 720

Finished Goods (400 units)
From opening work in progress (100 units)

Cost brought forward	240	
Cost to complete [40 × R1]	40	
		280
Goods started and completed during the period (300 × R3)		900
Transferred to finished goods		R1 180

Closing work in progress (200 units)

Materials (200 × R2)	400	
Labour (140 × R1)	140	
		540
Costs accounted for		R1 720

Applying Weighted average:

	Units	Materials	Labour
Goods completed	400	400	400
Closing WIP	200	200	140
Equivalent units		600	540

Costs to account for

	Materials	Labour
From WIP bfwd	190	50
Current	1 000	480
	R1 190	R530
Cost per equivalent unit	±R1,98	±R0,98

Finished goods (400 units)
400 × 2,96   R1 185
Closing work in progress (200 units)
  Materials   [200 × 1,98]   397
  Labour   [140 × 0,98]   138
                                                                   535
                                                                R1 720

Spoilage

The concept of spoilage has already been dealt with under job costing. In process costing the concept does not change. Abnormal spoilage must be accounted for and written off in the income statement. Normal spoilage must be added to the cost of good production.

In calculating the equivalent units, the cost of abnormal spoilage must be calculated.

With normal spoilage, which ultimately finds its way into the cost of production, there are two alternatives. One is to ignore the normal spoilage completely, with the result that the cost of that spoilage will automatically be spread over all the output of that period. Alternatively, equivalent units may be allocated to the normal spoilage and the amount calculated for normal spoilage is then added to the cost of the good production.

Spoilage may be treated as occurring at the point of detection or at the point of inspection.

These methods of costing products i.e. job and process costing, are part of what is known as full costing, also known as total costing or absorption costing. This contrasts with marginal costing or contribution costing or variable costing, which is dealt with in a later chapter.

QUESTIONS

7.1 Identify the features that distinguish job costing from process costing.

7.2 Jasal Ltd manufactures products A and B in the Mel department. Expenses incurred in the Mel department for week 35 were:

Rent	560
Salaries and wages	2 300
Electricity	350
Materials	16 000
Maintenance	4 500

Products A and B and made on the same machines and by the same staff. The only difference between the two is that A uses twice as much material but only half the time taken by product B.

You are required to calculate the cost of each of the products for week 35. No unexpected spoilage or downtime occurred and 1 500 units of A and 3 000 units of B were manufactured.

You are also required to state the basis on which you have allocated the various costs and to determine the unit cost of each product.

7.3 The accountant and production manager of Fancy Fences Ltd were out of town for the week. The assistant production manager had begun production of a new slab called SE1. The new slab was unique in that the water contained a white dye giving the vibracrete fence a permanent white surface. It was only after the workers had started mixing the cement that the assistant realised that he did not know how much dye to add to the mixture. The bookkeeper supplied him with the file on slab SE1 and from this he learned the following information.

1. Selling price to subcontractor = R400 per batch of 100 slabs
2. Mark-up on cost: $33\frac{1}{3}\%$
3. Production batch size: 50
4. Direct labour hours: 40
5. Standard cost per direct labour hour: R1,75
6. Cement per batch: 100 kgs
7. Cement cost per kg: R0,60
8. Overhead allocation base: R0,25 per direct labour hour
9. Cost of dye: R1 per litre.

REQUIRED

Calculate the number of litres of dye that must be added to the water when mixing the cement for one batch of SE1 slabs.

7.4 In your capacity as a financial consultant you have been approached by Major Kurt Johannsen, a retired pilot of the Danish Air Force. Major Johannsen intends submitting a tender for the carriage of passengers by air from Johannesburg to a casino that is close to completion in a neighbouring country.

He asks you to calculate a price per economy and first-class seat for return flights to and from the casino for a period of one year. For every seat that is unoccupied the carrier will be paid the normal fare by the casino.

You thereafter assemble the following information regarding costs. An aircraft can be chartered from Boeing in the USA at a flat annual rental of R2,5 million. The fuel cost is calculated at a fixed cost of R4 000 plus a variable cost of R3 per passenger per return flight. Major Johannsen will be one of the pilots and the total fixed salary account for another two pilots and the crew will amount to R154 000 in the next year. The processing and administration costs per ticket have been negotiated with a reservation agency at R10 per ticket. Other variable costs (mainly meals and drinks) have been calculated at R15 per person per economy return flight and R25 per person per first class return flight.

The Boeing to be used conforms to the tender specifications. It has 200 economy passenger seats and 40 first-class passenger seats. There will be two return flights each day.

Major Johannsen feels that as the space needed for a first-class seat is 50% more than that needed for an economy seat the contribution per first-class seat should be 50% higher than the contribution per economy seat. Major Johannsen would like the net income of the venture to be at least R120 000.

The percentage of occupied seats on an aircraft flight is termed the load factor.

REQUIRED

Calculate the tender price of the economy and first-class seats.

8 Contract Costing

A particular type of job is the long term contract, the accounting for which is known as contract costing. Generally contract costing is used in the case of a relatively large project lasting more than a year. It is most frequently used when an enterprise embarks on the construction of an item such as a bridge, a building or a ship.

A contract is simply a large job and the principles of job costing may be applied. A contract account (job card) is maintained and attracts costs in much the same way as discussed under job costing. However, due to their size, construction contracts last for a lengthy period. This gives rise to one of the major problems in dealing with contracts viz. the recognition of income. The question is whether it is equitable to wait till the completion of the contract before recognising income, or whether it is fair to say that income is generated during the period of the contract and not only on completion.

Let us look at the life of the contract. The contractees will decide they need something built, for example a shopping complex. Architects are commissioned to design a project, tenders will be called for and the contractees will approve a tender, according to the price and the reputation of the contractor. During the course of the contract the architect will periodically issue a certificate of work completed i.e. the value of the project completed to date. This 'value' (less amounts previously paid) is paid to the contractor after deduction of a retention—an amount retained against any defects. Once the contract is finally completed to the specifications laid down and to the architect's satisfaction, and the agreed retention period has passed, any amounts still owing are paid to the contractor.

This chapter is concerned with accounting for the contract in the books of the contractor whose tender is accepted; each contract may be regarded as a cost centre or job, costs are charged to each contract.

We will examine some of the costs in contract costing. These are similar to those in job costing, but they may have one or two peculiarities worth noting.

CONTRACT COSTS

Materials

Materials may be purchased specifically for a contract or they may be issued to the contract from central stores. In either case they are charged to the contract, either directly from the supplier or via central stores.

Labour

Most labour will be direct; obvious examples are the labourer on the site, the nightwatchman who looks after the site, the foreman on the site, and the site accountant. Some labour may be indirect, such as the truck drivers. The main point is that the parameters of the cost centre in the contract are much wider, so costs that are normally indirect in job costing may be direct in the case of a contract.

Plant

Plant may be charged to a contract in one of two ways. The cost or book value of the plant may be charged to the contract, and at the end of the contract the value, or selling price, if sold, is credited to the contract. Alternatively, a plant hire rate may be determined and charged to the contract. The charge may be on a time basis, either daily, hourly, weekly, or monthly. In other words, the contractor owns the plant and he hires the plant out to his various contracts as if hired from an outsider at predetermined rates.

Overheads

These may be allocated to the contract on some equitable absorption rate. It must be noted that the overheads usually form a very small portion of the total costs of a contract so that the particular method of absorption used is unlikely to have a significant impact on the total contract cost.

PROFIT DETERMINATION

While the contract has been in progress, the contractor has had to bear all the expenses and the contractee has received something of value. Thus the architect from time to time issues a certificate of work completed, i.e. he certifies that work to a specific value has been completed and the contractor is entitled to payment of that amount. However, the contractee does not pay the whole value of work completed to the contractor.

A percentage agreed on beforehand is withheld as a guarantee for faulty work or failure to complete the contract on time. This retention is paid to the contractor after the contract is satisfactorily completed.

At the end of the contract, the contractor adds up the expenses, deducts from this his fee and so determines whether a profit or a loss has been made on the contract. Earlier it was said that a contract usually takes more than a year to complete: so what is done at the balance sheet date in the case of uncompleted contracts? Can we take a profit on an uncompleted contract? In this context let us consider the concepts of prudence and matching.

Prudence requires conservatism, so profits are not recognised until they are reasonably certain. Matching requires matching revenue with expenditure. Matching and prudence may be in conflict. If we have a conflict, prudence will take precedence.

The contractor can decide as a policy to take profits only when contracts are complete, ignoring matching and applying prudence strictly. It may even be argued that trying to determine some method of taking profits during the currency of the contract is pointless because results will even themselves out over the years. Each year some contracts will be finishing as others start, so by waiting for them all to finish we will end up with the same total result over time. This may be true, but, it may not be conceptually correct. Most businesses at some time or another have some contract that is much larger than the type of contract they normally enter into, which may distort their reported profits considerably.

On the other hand profits can be recognised during the course of the contract. This may be done by calculating the profit according to the matching concept and then applying prudence. There are two general methods of taking the profit on the matching concept. These are known as the work certified method, and the percentage of completion method.

The Work Certified Method

This method of accounting is based on utilising the certificates of work completed. In other words, the contract is credited with the amounts reflected in the certificates. The cost of the work certified is deducted, thereby yielding the profit to date. Prudence would dictate that account should be taken of the amount of the retention deducted in reporting the profit. Alternatively, the proportion that the cash retention bears to work certified would be applied to the profit, and this amount deducted. This latter approach is the less prudent of the two.

The Percentage of Completion Method

This method of accounting is based on estimating the total costs and the profit of the contract and applying this to the amount of work certified.

A certain amount of work has been certified, the total estimated contract price is known as well as the total estimated profit, so this proportion of profit is taken. Alternatively the cost of the work to date as a proportion of the total estimated costs is applied to the total estimated profit. The difference between these two methods is that the former is based on the relationship that the work done to date bears to the total contract price i.e. the total selling price. The latter is based on the relationship that the work done to date bears to the total costs to be incurred.

Either of these proportions is then applied to the total estimated profit to determine the amount of profit to be reported.

The percentage of completion method is more appropriately used late in the contract when the estimates can be made with a reasonable degree of accuracy.

Prudence can be applied to the profit calculated by any of the methods described in one of two ways. Either deduct the retention, i.e. the amount not received in cash will not be regarded as the profit. Or, a slightly less conservative approach, is to reduce the profit by applying to it the proportion of cash received to work certified.

Some writers have suggested that with the work certified method a further provision against possible losses or unexpected expenditure should be made. The amount suggested is a third of the profits. This has no theoretical justification, but may be prudent. Clearly this provision is unnecessary with the percentage of completion method. As this is utilised late in the contract any possible losses or extra costs would be accounted for in the estimate of the total contract profit.

SUMMARY—IMPACT OF MATCHING AND PRUDENCE

Work certified method

Matching		*Prudence*	
Work certified	XXX	Calculated profit	XXX
Less cost of work		Less retention	XXX
certified	XXX		
Calculated profit	XXX	Reported profit	XXX

$$\text{OR} \qquad \text{Calculated profit} \times \frac{\text{cash received}}{\text{work certified}}$$
$$= \text{reported profit}$$

Percentage of completion method

$$\frac{\text{work certified}}{\text{contract price}} \times \text{estimated total profit} \qquad \text{as above}$$

$$= \text{calculated profit}$$

OR

$$\frac{\text{costs to date}}{\text{estimated total costs}} \times \text{estimated total profit} \qquad \text{as above}$$

$$= \text{calculated profit}$$

Illustrative Example

Contract price	R100 000
Cost to date	60 000
Estimated additional cost to completion	10 000
Work certified	75 000
Retention	5 000
Cost of work certified	50 000

WORK CERTIFIED METHOD

Work certified	R75 000	
Cost of work certified	50 000	
Calculated profit	25 000	
Retention	5 000	
Reported profit	R20 000	OR

$$\underset{\text{profit}}{\text{Calculated}} \times \frac{\text{cash received}}{\text{work certified}} \quad \text{i.e. } 25\,000 \times \frac{70\,000}{75\,000}$$

i.e. reported profit = R23 333

PERCENTAGE OF COMPLETION METHOD

Contract price		100 000	
Cost to date	60 000		
Additional costs to complete	10 000	70 000	
Estimated total profit		R30 000	

Based on contract price:

$$\frac{\text{work certified}}{\text{contract price}} \times \text{estimated total profit} = \text{calculated profit}$$

$\dfrac{75\,000}{100\,000} \times 30\,000$	= 22 500	
less retention	5 000	
reported profit	R17 500	OR

$$\text{calculated profit} \times \frac{\text{cash received}}{\text{work certified}}$$

$$22\ 500 \times \frac{70\ 000}{75\ 000} = \text{reported profit} \qquad = \underline{\underline{\text{R21 000}}}$$

Based on cost:

$$\frac{\text{cost to date}}{\text{estimated total cost}} \times \text{estimated total profit} = \frac{\text{calculated}}{\text{profit}}$$

$$\frac{60\ 000}{70\ 000} \times 30\ 000 \qquad\qquad\qquad = 25\ 714$$

less retention   5 000

reported profit $\underline{\underline{\text{R20 714}}}$ OR

$$\text{calculated profit} \times \frac{\text{cash received}}{\text{work certified}}$$

$$25\ 714 \times \frac{70\ 000}{75\ 000} = \text{reported profit} \qquad = \underline{\underline{\text{R24 000}}}$$

This example clearly illustrates the different reported profits that may result from the same basic information.

WORK-IN-PROGRESS

There are several methods by which the figure for work-in-progress can be derived.

Using the information in the above example, these methods are illustrated, using the reported profit of R17 500.

Contract a/c

Costs	60 000	Work certified	75 000
Profit	17 500	Balance	2 500
	R77 500		R77 500
Balance	2 500		

Contract	Debtors	Retention	
70 000		5 000	

Balance on contract account	R2 500
Retention	5 000
	R7 500

Disclosure on the balance sheet can take several forms, including the following 3 examples:

1. *Current assets*
    Work in progress   7 500
    Contract debtors   70 000

2. *Current assets*
    Work in progress   2 500
    Contract debtors   70 000
    Retention   5 000

3. *Current assets*
    Work in progress   77 500 [cost, 60 000 + profit, 17 500]
    Retention   5 000

    Current liabilities
    Work certified   75 000

Methods 1 and 2 are the most common.

However, the effect on the balance sheet will be markedly different using example 3.

Consequently one can appreciate the difficulty of analysing financial statements in the light of several different yet acceptable bases of accounting for contracts.

QUESTIONS

8.1 Contract costing may be likened to job costing. Explain why.

What is the fundamental difference between job and contract costing and what is the impact of this difference?

8.2 Watters Construction was formed early in 1989 by the accountant and works foreman of a prominent public construction company. The builders holiday commenced on 14 December 1989 and the financial year of the firm ends on 31 December 1989. The firm was awarded three building contracts during 1989 and the results of these contracts are as follows:

CONTRACT

Details	A	B	C	Total
Work certified 14.12.89	800 000	400 000	200 000	1 400 000
Payments received 31.12.89	800 000	400 000	200 000	1 400 000
Percentage of completion	90%	50%	20%	
Labour costs allowed	160 000	200 000	50 000	410 000
Labour hours allowed	80 000	66 667	12 500	159 167
Actual direct labour costs	240 000	200 000	50 000	490 000
Actual direct labour hours	80 000	100 000	12 500	192 500
Material costs	200 000	100 000	125 000	425 000
Variable overhead				200 000
Fixed overhead				100 000
Selling and administrative				100 000

You are given the following information:

1. Material costs, variable overhead, fixed overhead and selling and administrative expenses were all equal to budgeted expenditure.

2. Profits are only recognised on contracts that have a percentage of completion of 50% or greater.

3. The works foreman is of the opinion that the variable overhead should be allocated to contracts on the basis of actual direct labour hours as he feels this expense to be clearly correlated to actual time spent working on site.

4. The accountant is of the opinion that the variable overhead should be allocated to contracts on the basis of labour costs allowed as he feels this expense to be closely correlated to the levels of skills allowed prior to the commencement of the contract.

5. The labour costs and labour hours allowed are those amounts allowed to 14 December 1989.

REQUIRED

1. Calculate the total cash flow generated by contracts A, B and C for the period ended 31 December 1989. Assume that all expenses were paid for in cash immediately upon purchase and ignore taxation.

2. Calculate the net income before taxation with the variable overhead allocated on the basis suggested by the works foreman.

3. Calculate the net income before taxation with the variable overhead allocated on the basis suggested by the accountant.

4. If the fixed overhead were to be allocated and inventoried would this be consistent with the variable or the absorption costing approach? Would this increase or decrease the net incomes calculated in 2 and 3 above?

5. If the accountant was considering allocating selling and administrative expenses on the basis suggested by him state with which of the following basic accounting principles this idea be consistent or inconsistent:
   — matching
   — historical cost
   — going concern
   — prudence

In the light of your answer to this section, state which approach you feel is correct.

6. In this situation profits are only recognised on contracts that are 50% or more complete. If the firm had had numerous contracts in progress at the year end, and it purposefully wished to increase profits, everything else held constant, would it increase or decrease the 50% rule?

7. From the labour and material amounts given, state which contract is:

   (a) the most labour intensive
   (b) the most material intensive
   (c) which contract was budgeted to use the most skilled labour
   (d) which contract had the largest deviation from the budgeted amounts.

9 Marginal Costing

Marginal costing is of use to management in fulfilling its decision-making functions particularly when faced with alternative courses of action. Marginal costing is sometimes also referred to as direct or variable costing. Before discussing marginal costing and its uses and implications it would help to understand the meaning of contribution.

CONTRIBUTION AND BREAK-EVEN

Contribution is the difference between the selling price of an item and its variable cost. It may also be expressed as the contribution that the sale of an item makes towards fixed costs and profits. If an item sells for R10 and has variable costs of R6, every time an item is sold, R4 goes into the company coffers. This R4 will first be applied towards meeting the overheads and once all overheads are covered, a profit will result. More attention will be paid later in this chapter to the uses of contribution as an aid to decision-making.

In some of the previous chapters we arrived at a valuation of stock by allocating all costs and all overheads to the items produced. By using the marginal costing approach, fixed costs are not allocated to the cost of the items produced and are not carried in stock, but are written off when incurred. This is in contrast to the absorption costing approach where all costs are allocated to the products.

The following illustrates the use of marginal costing in a simple decision-making process.

A business may consist solely of a chocolate vending machine. Each chocolate costs the business 40c and is sold for 50 cents. The rent of the machine is R100 per month and the contribution from each chocolate sold is 10c (50c − 40c). How many chocolates must be sold for the business to break even? Or to put it another way: if you were offered the opportunity of installing a chocolate vending machine on your premises, you would want to know how many chocolates you would have to sell not to suffer a loss.

In this case we can clearly see that every chocolate sold results in a 10 cents contribution. We need to cover R100 fixed costs (the rent paid for the vending machine), therefore we need to sell 1 000 chocolates (i.e. R100 divided by 10c). So now we can consider whether we have a fair chance of selling 1 000 chocolates a month or not. We now have something concrete to help us decide whether to install the machine.

If we were interested in knowing the rand value of sales we require, we could then consider the contribution per rand of sales. For every rand of sales we make we are going to make a contribution of 20c, as R1 represents the sale of 2 chocolates and every chocolate makes 10c contribution. We are going to make 20c per rand so we have to sell R500 [100 ÷ 0,20] worth of chocolates to break even (i.e. to meet our fixed costs). This is consistent with the previous answer where we established we had to sell 1 000 chocolates. 1 000 chocolates at 50c each equals R500.

If we decide that any venture we enter into must yield a profit of R20 before we are interested, we would want to know how many chocolates we need to sell before we reach this level. What we want to know is not that we avoid making a loss on this vending machine but that we make our desired level of profit. If what we want is to cover our fixed costs of R100 and make a desired level of profit of R20, this then forms the numerator. The denominator remains the same at 10 cents per chocolate or 20 cents per rand. So we now know we need to sell 1 200 chocolates [120 ÷ 0,20] or R600 of chocolates to achieve our desired profit.

SENSITIVITY ANALYSIS

One of the most important factors in the various management accounting techniques is that they allow for the application of sensitivity analysis. Sensitivity analysis involves considering how sensitive the figures or information we have used are to change. In other words, in the case of the vending machine we could say we have to sell 1 000 chocolates to break even and the figures are fairly certain. We know the rent will be R100 per month. We know our contribution will be 10 cents a chocolate, this is also fairly certain.

You will appreciate that most businesses are more complex. It will be more difficult to determine exactly what the fixed costs are going to be, or what the variable costs are, or in fact that those figures will remain at those levels. We can see by changing certain figures how susceptible we are to change. Assume we think the vending machine may in fact cost R105. How will this affect our decision? We now know we need to sell 1 050 chocolates to break even rather than 1 000.

The critical aspect of sensitivity analysis is whether the decision will change with changes in the variables.

An important use of sensitivity analysis arises when a desired profit is required. By applying sensitivity one can then see by how much sales would need to drop before we lose our profit and go into a loss situation. For example to achieve a profit of R20 on the vending machine at a fixed cost level of R100 we needed to sell 1 200 chocolates each month. We could then say by how much sales would have to drop before we incur a loss. We can determine this to be a drop of more than 200 chocolates a month. This may or may not be considered risky to the business. Or we could ask, should the cost of chocolates go up by 1 cent, what would this do to our profits? Would a small increase in cost create a proportionately large decrease in profits or vice versa? Or do the costs and profits move consistently with or apart from each other?

These relationships may be illustrated graphically:

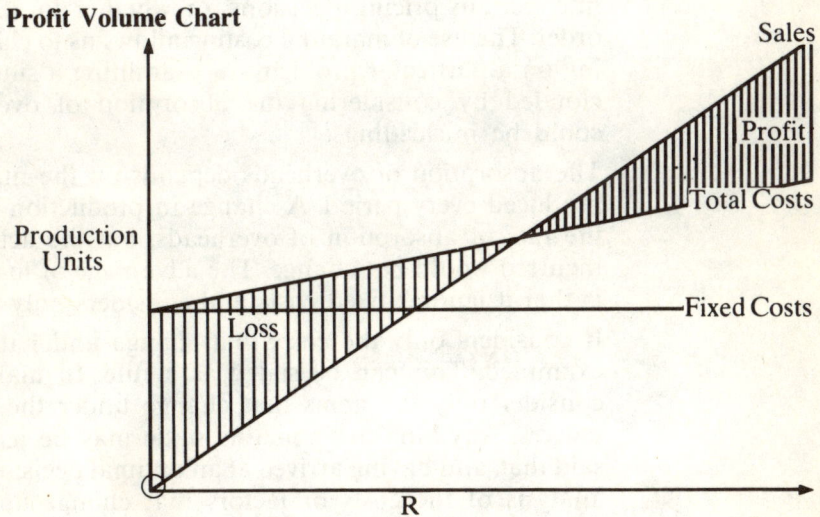

Profit Volume Chart

Break Even Chart

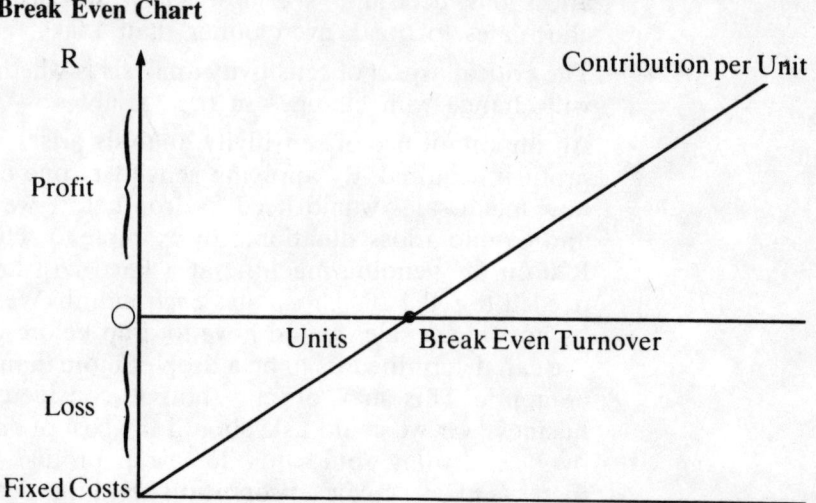

MARGINAL DECISION MAKING

The types of decision where marginal costing is useful, include the make or buy, adding a new product line, dropping a product line, certain pricing decisions, or whether to accept a special order. The use of marginal costing allows us to clarify our thinking on a particular problem. In examining a situation it is not clouded by considering the absorption of overheads which could be misleading.

The absorption of overheads depends on the number of units produced every period. A change in production would change the rate of absorption of overheads, but the actual overheads incurred would not change. The advantage of marginal costing is that it ignores fixed costs and considers only variable costs.

It considers only the costs that change under the alternatives examined. This can be stated as a rule. In making decisions consider only the items that change under the various alternatives. Anything that remains static may be ignored. Having said that, and having arrived at an optimal decision based on an analysis of the costs or factors that change under the alternatives, one must then always remember to consider the qualitative factors. These very often have a more important bearing on the situation than the numerical analysis in isolation.

For example a company is considering importing a special lathe which will produce a new kind of metal bearing, expected to sell at R20 and attract variable costs of R15 per unit. Fixed costs are expected to be R10 000 per year.

A quantitative analysis indicates the following:

Contribution   R5 per unit
Breakeven   2 000 units

Assuming the company expects to be able to sell 3 000 units per year, the venture is clearly profitable. However other factors to be considered may include:

The entry into the market by competitors.
The development of substitute products.
Are there sufficient trained operators available?
Are spares and back-up service for the lathe available?
Alternative uses of capital invested.
Effect on existing product lines.
Use of lathe for other products.
Security of raw material supply.

Limiting Factors

We looked at the contribution per unit and arrived at certain decisions. However, at times this can indicate the wrong decision because if we have limiting factors then we need to look at the contribution per limiting factor and not the contribution per unit. A limiting factor is some factor or item which limits the number of units that may be produced or the number of units that may be sold.

The contribution expected to be made should be looked at in relation to any limiting factors, as those factors will determine the profits that we can achieve.

For example, if we have 10 kilograms of material available and with those 10 kilograms we can produce either 1 item of product A which gives a contribution of R20 or we can produce 5 items of product B which gives a contribution of R6 each, which product should be made?

If we examine the contribution per unit it indicates a preference for product A because that gives a contribution of R20 as opposed to R6 for product B. But we have a limit of materials available. We have only 10 kilos of material. With 10 kilos of material we would either get a contribution of R20 for product A or a contribution of R30 (R6 × 5 units) for product B. In terms of the contribution per limiting factor we would find that, since the limiting factor is material, for every kilo of material there is a contribution of R2 (20 ÷ 10) for product A. In the case of product B for every kilo of material there is a contribution of R12.

The limiting factor can take various forms, it could be the limit of a type of material, different types of material, labour availability, different grades of labour, or finance available, floor space, sales, manpower; the list is endless.

The following examples illustrate some of the areas where marginal costing techniques aid in the decision-making process.

Make or Buy

Morb Ltd buys 5 000 units per year of a component used in its production lines. These units cost R8 each.

The management of Morb is considering making the component in its factory. Costs to be incurred are expected to be as follows:

100 gm material @ R10 per kg
2 hrs labour @ R1 per hour
Variable overheads @ 50c per hour
Depreciation of machinery R15 000 per annum
Rent allocated for factory floor R1 000 per annum
Foreman to supervise production R10 000 per annum

Costs to make:	
Materials 5 000 × R1	R5 000
Labour 5 000 × R2	10 000
Variable overheads 5 000 × R1	5 000
	20 000
Depreciation	15 000
Foreman	10 000
Rent irrelevant — incurred whether make or buy	NIL
Total cost to make 5 000 units	R45 000
Total cost to buy 5 000 units — 5 000 × R8	R40 000

∴ continue to buy.

Special Order

Sord Ltd produces and sells sods and has been approached by Lazy Ltd to supply a special order of 10 000 units of sods for a gimmick line which it intends marketing. Sord has ample spare capacity in its factory.

Sods usually sell for R5 but Lazy is offering R4 per sod.

Costs in the sod factory are:

Materials	R2,00 per unit
Labour	R1,00 per unit
Variable overhead	R0,75 per unit
Fixed costs	R20 000 per annum

Fixed costs are irrelevant as they are incurred whether or not the additional sods are produced.

Variable costs	R3,75
Price offered	R4,00
Contribution	0,25 per unit

∴ increased profit by accepting the order

$$10\ 000 \times 0,25 = R2\ 500$$

Before accepting the order Sord Ltd must carefully consider the effect this may have on its regular customers. Other qualitative factors must be considered such as alternative uses for the factory space and whether Sord Ltd could use the facilities to increase its own production at its higher normal selling price.

In the simple cases above it was stated that fixed costs do not change under the alternatives. Very often in practice there is a change in the fixed costs. Care must be exercised in 'ignoring' fixed costs for there is a danger that they may be 'forgotten'. In the extreme this could result in using a factory's entire capacity with production that yields a contribution but is not sufficient to cover fixed costs.

With marginal costing, as with any decision-making process it is essential to adopt a broad 'eyes-open' approach to the numerical analysis undertaken.

QUESTIONS

9.1 The contribution approach is frequently used in making decisions.

REQUIRED

1. Explain this approach.
2. What are its advantages?
3. What are the dangers?

9.2 Albert Company sells its products for R25 per unit. Variable costs of manufacture are R10 per unit, and fixed manufacturing costs amount to R60 000 per annum. It costs R5 to sell each unit while fixed administrative and selling expenses amount to R24 000 per annum.

REQUIRED

1. Calculate the breakeven point in both units and rands.
2. How many units must be sold to earn a profit of R50 000?
3. If variable manufacturing costs were to increase by 20%, by how many units would the breakeven point increase?

9.3 Stonefarm Investments Ltd is a company engaged in pumping diamonds from the seabed.

The process is as follows: Divers are sent down with suction equipment which pumps the seabed into 1 000 kilogram tanks. These tanks are then taken ashore and the contents of the tanks are processed in order to separate the diamonds from the remainder of the seabed. Each tank yields 30 carats of diamonds which are sold for R90 000.

The costs up to the stage where the diamonds are separated from the remainder of the seabed are, for each tank:

(a) Fixed costs: Divers' fees   R800
                  Wages   100
                  Depreciation   100
                                                  R1 000

(b) Variable operating costs: R2 per kilogram of seabed pumped into a tank.

The remainder of the seabed after the diamonds have been extracted is then ground into a fine powder known as Gobabis Granules, which is used as a paint additive. The cost of grinding is R4 per kilogram and the Granules sell for R10 per kilogram. For all practical purposes the weight of the seabed, after extracting the diamonds, can be regarded as 1 000 kilograms, for 30 carats of diamonds weigh only a few grams.

The company has now developed a process whereby, instead of simply selling the seabed as Gobabis Granules, the seabed is processed further and separated into two products, sea creatures and Gobabis Granules, in the ratio of 1:2. The cost of separating the two products is R10 per kilogram of input; there is a loss during the process of 10% of the input. The sea creatures are then further processed at a cost of R4 per kilogram and sold for R30 per kilogram to the local farmers as Frankle's Fishy Fertiliser. Gobabis Granules, which as a result of the separation of the sea creatures are now of a better quality, can be sold without further processing for R13 per kilogram (i.e. the grinding process is no longer necessary).

REQUIRED

Advise the company whether the seabed should be processed to produce only Gobabis Granules or whether the seabed should be processed to produce both Frankle's Fishy Fertiliser and Gobabis Granules.

9.4 Rubber Ltd, a Cape Town company, is engaged in the manufacture and supply of widgets. The company is keen to expand its operation to the Transvaal, and has retained Terry Poulle as its agent in the area.

Poulle will receive a retainer of R46 000 p.a. plus a commission of 10% of sales.

The widgets sell for R40 each. The variable costs of manufacture are R10 per unit. Fixed manufacturing costs at the factory in Cape Town amount to R100 000 per annum regardless of the level of production.

Railage from the factory in Cape Town, where the goods are manufactured, to Johannesburg amounts to R5 per unit.

In addition to his retainer and commission, Poulle will receive a motor car costing R40 000. The car is expected to last 4 years and have a resale value of R4 000 at the end of the 4th year. Other costs of running the car are estimated to be variable costs of 40c per kilometre, and fixed costs (excluding depreciation) are calculated to be 60c per kilometre. It is estimated that Poulle will travel 50 000 kilometres per annum in the course of his job.

The Transvaal operation will have 10% of existing administration expenses allocated to it. Total administration expenses are R60 000 per annum.

REQUIRED

Determine the number of units that must be sold annually for the Transvaal operation to break even.

9.5 Luap Gropes is the editor of *Gib Dele*, a magazine with a small circulation, mostly amongst the intelligentsia.

Luap has received an article from an outspoken student which condemns the business ethics of certain well-known companies, one of which, at R500 per month, is a big advertiser in the magazine.

Luap fears that publication of the article may cause the advertiser to withdraw his support for the magazine. On the other hand a far greater number of copies are expected to be sold this month on account of the article.

Each copy sold generates a contribution of R0,20.

REQUIRED

List the factors Luap should consider in deciding whether to print the article or not.

9.6 Refer to question 7.4

Your tender has been accepted. As a result of the negligence of one of the pilots you ascertain that the Boeing in use will require repairs that will be carried out over a period of 14 days during the coming month of August. A penalty clause in the tender states that the carrier will pay the casino R10 000 per day that an aircraft is not in use. A similar Boeing can be hired from SAA for R181 000 for the 14 day period. You can reliably estimate that the load factor will be 80% during the 14 day period. Advise Major Johannsen as to the most preferable course of action.

9.7 Bruler Ltd has asked you to assist in arriving at a decision whether to continue manufacturing a part or to buy it from an outside supplier.

The part, named Blime, is used in some of the finished products of the company. Blimes are manufactured in the machining department. You are aware of the following:

1. Total costs of the machining department in a year during which 5 000 Blimes are required are:

Materials	R67 500
Direct labour	50 000
Indirect labour	20 000
Electricity	8 500
Depreciation	10 000
Rates and insurance	8 000
Fringe benefits	9 800
Other	5 000
	R178 800

2. The lowest quote received for the purchase of Blimes from an outside supplier is R8 per unit. If the Blimes are purchased certain equipment would be scrapped for no value. Such equipment is now being depreciated at R2 000 per year.

3. The following machining department costs are directly traceable to the Blimes and would be eliminated if the Blimes were purchased.

Materials	R17 500
Direct labour	28 000
Indirect labour	6 000
Electricity	300
Other	500

4. Scrapping the equipment will reduce insurance by R1 000 per year.

5. Fringe benefits are assumed to be variable with labour costs.

6. If the Blimes are purchased the following additional costs will be incurred:

    Railage   50c per unit
    Indirect labour for handling etc.   R5 000 per year

REQUIRED

1. Calculate whether it will be more profitable to make or buy the Blimes.

2. List the qualitative factors to be considered before a decision is made.

10 Budgeting

A student does not merely arrive at a university, sit down in a lecture theatre and simply expect that following this haphazard procedure will eventually result in a desired qualification. Hopefully the student would embark on a university career with the intention of acquiring a particular qualification. To achieve this the student will have considered the courses to be studied, the number of years involved, prerequisites for courses, scheduling the time-table to avoid clashes, the course fees and the cost of books and accessories, housing, accommodation fees, and all other pertinent factors.

In other words successful completion of a project requires a co-ordinated plan of action. Budgeting can be described as the co-ordination of all resources required to carry out a desired plan. As in the case of the student a business needs to consider and plan where it is going and how it intends getting there.

A particular budget cycle is usually part of a business' long range goals. It is the expression, in numerical terms, of the courses of action to be undertaken over the ensuing budget cycle in the attempt to satisfy those goals. Budgets are not always expressed in monetary terms. For example, labour budgets may be expressed in labour hours, stock budgets may be expressed in quantities of stock items.

Most business entities have some type of formal budget process, in fact, some produce budgets covering several years. Because all budgets have some degree of uncertainty they are normally revised on an on-going basis as situations change.

Take the case of a budget covering periods 1 to 3. At the end of period 1 a budget for periods 2 to 4 may be compiled and additional information which comes to hand relating to periods 2 and 3 would be taken into account and the existing budgets for those periods would be suitably revised. This is referred to as roll-over budgeting.

Since budgets are based on assumptions as to future conditions, such as the inflation rate or demand, some firms prepare budgets which cover ranges of possibilities. They take into account different changes to the assumptions on which their budget is based, which is often referred to as sensitivity analysis. This means that if conditions change within the range of possibilities considered, the likely effect would already be illustrated in the budget.

Budgeting forms part of the planning and the control functions in an organisation. The budget process assists management in achieving its stated objective, e.g. the attainment of a certain profit or a desired return on investment.

This is achieved by the planning function and by the control function, whereby deviations from a budget are highlighted and investigated and where feasible corrective action is taken. A budget should also motivate people to perform in the best interests of the business. Motivation is often best achieved by involving the staff, who are responsible for the various elements of the budget, in its establishment.

BUDGET PREPARATION

A sales forecast is usually the first step in preparing a budget. Following the sales forecast many expense items, such as production costs, which are a function of units sold, can be more readily forecast. Others, such as rent or administrative salaries, are fixed. This is not to imply that expenses should not be separately budgeted. Indeed they should be critically estimated and evaluated, yet it is true that once sales are known it is much easier to budget for expenses.

Forecasting is the process of estimating a level of activity. This may be done on a subjective or on an objective basis.

Subjective bases include:

Personal estimates — an individual tries to predict.
Group estimates — a group collectively predicts.
Delphi technique — a process whereby a group individually predict and revise predictions after exposure to the predictions from the other group members.

Objective bases include:

Simple average — the prediction is based on the simple average of past actual data.
Weighted average — as for simple average except that the past data is weighted.
Exponential smoothing — a mathematical technique which weights current data and all past data as a prediction base.
Regression analysis — a statistical technique whereby a prediction may be made based on a trend which has been established by correlation.

Having estimated sales, one is in a position to estimate:

Production requirements — raw materials, labour, production facilities, stock holding, etc.

Marketing requirements — advertising, sales force, etc.

Administration — information processing, finance etc.

It should be noted that production is dependent on sales, marketing has an effect on sales as has research and development, but administration is dependent on all the above.

BUDGET COMPILATION

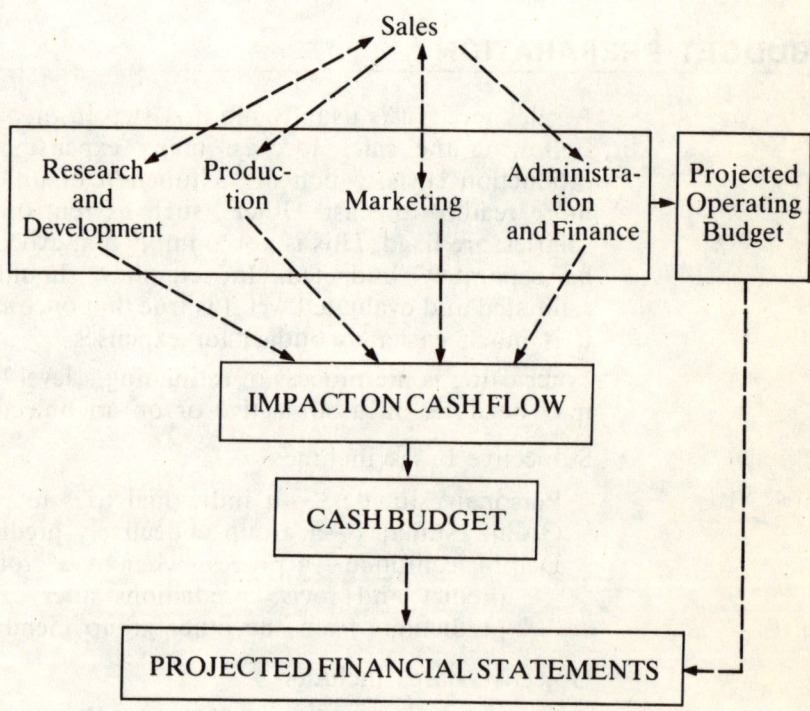

Illustrative Example

Mub (Pty) Ltd has collected the following projected information regarding its proposed activities:

	Sales (Units)
December	11 000 (actual)
January	9 000 (estimated)
February	16 000 („)
March	18 000 („)
April	18 000 („)
May	20 000 („)
June	20 000 („)

Each unit has the following production requirements:

Material: 3 kg um at R2/kg

2 kg ub at R5/kg

Labour: 1 hr at R4/hr

Variable overhead is incurred @ R1 per labour hour.

Fixed manufacturing overhead is expected to be R40 000 per month.

Variable selling expenses are R2 per unit. Fixed selling expenses and administration overhead are expected to be R10 000 and R15 000 respectively.

Mub considers it necessary to hold sufficient finished goods for one months' sales. In addition it intends to hold sufficient raw material to cater for the following two months' production.

Proceeds of sales are expected to be received as follows:

80%	30 days credit
18%	cash (after 10% discount)
2%	bad debts not collected

The selling price is R50 per unit.

Mub has negotiated credit of 60 days on the purchase of materials it uses. All other expenses are paid for in the month incurred.

Manufacturing overhead includes R5 000 per month for depreciation.

A new machine was installed at the beginning of January at a cost of R100 000. This has to be paid for at the end of March. Mub is required to make a provisional tax payment of R500 000 in February. Stock is valued on a FIFO basis and finished goods include only variable production costs. There is no work in progress at the end of any month. Cash on hand at the beginning of January is expected to be R4 000.

Operating and cash budgets for the period January to March may now be prepared.

MATERIAL USAGE

The value of stock on hand at the beginning of January can be calculated on the following basis:

Finished goods 9 000 units (sales for January kept on hand) valued at variable manufacturing cost.

Materials:	Um	[R2 × 3 kg × 9 000]	54 000
	Ub	[R5 × 2 kg × 9 000]	90 000
Labour:		[R4 × 1 hr × 9 000]	36 000
Variable overhead		[R1 × 1 hr × 9 000]	9 000
			R189 000

Similarly projected finished goods on hand at 31st March will be:

18 000 units @ variable manufac-
turing cost of R21/unit i.e.   R378 000

Raw material stock on hand at 1st January will be for the next two months' production.

i.e. production in January   16 000 units for sale in February
production in February   18 000 units for sale in March

34 000 units

To produce 34 000 units requires:

Um 34 000 × R2 × 3 kg	204 000
Ub 34 000 × R5 × 2 kg	340 000
Raw material on hand 1st January	R544 000

The raw material purchases for the period can now be projected:

	(units)	Um (3 kg/u)	Ub (2 kg/u)
Stock 1st January [16 000 + 18 000]	34 000	102 000	68 000
Used January	16 000	48 000	32 000
	18 000	54 000	36 000
January purchases for			
March production (April sales)	18 000	54 000	36 000
Stock 31st January	36 000	108 000	72 000
Used February	18 000	54 000	36 000
	18 000	54 000	36 000
February purchases for			
April production (May sales)	20 000	60 000	40 000
Stock 28th February	38 000	114 000	76 000
Used March	18 000	54 000	36 000
	20 000	60 000	40 000

March purchases for				
May production	(June sales)	20 000	60 000	40 000
Stock 31st March		40 000	120 000	80 000
Cost per kg			R2	R5
			R240 000	R400 000

In summary:

	UM	UB
Stock holding 1st January	R204 000	R340 000
Purchases January	108 000	180 000
February	120 000	200 000
March	120 000	200 000
	552 000	920 000
Stock 31st March	240 000	400 000
Cost of material used	R312 000	R520 000
	R832 000	

BUDGETED MANUFACTURING STATEMENT

The budgeted manufacturing statement may now be prepared. Note it will cover production during the 3 months January to March. This production is to provide stock for the 3 months February to April.

BUDGETED MANUFACTURING STATEMENT FOR THE 3 MONTHS ENDED 31 MARCH 01

Materials		
Stock 1st January		544 000
Purchases		928 000
		1 472 000
Stock 31st March		640 000
Material used		832 000
Labour [(16 000 + 18 000 + 18 000) × R4]		208 000
Prime cost		1 040 000
Overheads		
Variable [52 000 × R1]	52 000	
Fixed [R40 000 × 3]	120 000	172 000
Cost of manufacture		R1 212 000

BUDGETED TRADING AND INCOME STATEMENT

The budgeted trading and income statements will cover sales for the 3 months January to March.

BUDGETED TRADING AND INCOME STATEMENT FOR THE 3 MONTHS ENDED 31 MARCH 01

Sales [43 000 × R50]		2 150 000
Cost of sales		
Stock 1st January [9 000 × 21]	189 000	
Cost of manufacture	1 212 000	
	1 401 000	
Stock 31st March [18 000 × 21]	378 000	
		1 023 000
Gross Profit		1 127 000
Less: expenses		
variable selling [43 000 × 2]	86 000	
fixed selling	30 000	
administration	45 000	
bad debts [2% of 2 150 000]	43 000	
interest	2 110	
		206 110
Budgeted net income before taxation		R920 890

CASH BUDGET

CASH BUDGET FOR THE 3 MONTHS ENDING 31 MARCH 01

	January	February	March
Cash Inflows			
Sales — receipts from credit sales (80% of previous month	440 000	360 000	640 000
— cash receipts (18% of current month)	81 000	144 000	162 000
	521 000	504 000	802 000
Cash Outflows			
Material — Um	54 000	96 000	108 000
— Ub	90 000	160 000	180 000
Labour	64 000	72 000	72 000
Variable overhead	16 000	18 000	18 000
Fixed overhead — manufacturing	35 000	35 000	35 000
Variable selling cost	18 000	32 000	36 000
Fixed overhead — selling	10 000	10 000	10 000
— administration	15 000	15 000	15 000
Machinery purchased			100 000
Provisional tax payment		500 000	
	302 000	938 000	574 000

	January	February	March
Monthly Surplus/(Deficit)	219 000	(434 000)	228 000
Surplus/(Deficit) — brought forward	4 000	223 000	(213 110)
	223 000	(211 000)	14 890
Interest (1% per month)	—	(2 110)	—
Surplus/(Deficit) — carried forward	R223 000	R(213 110)	R14 890

Notes:

1. While fixed manufacturing overheads amount to R40 000 per month, the cash budget takes into account R35 000, thereby excluding R5 000 for depreciation which does not involve a flow of funds. Only the payment or receipt of cash on the purchase or sale of an asset would have a cash flow effect.

2. The bad debts are recorded in the budgeted income statement but do not form part of the cash budget as they do not constitute a flow of cash but rather a lack of cash flow.

3. Materials are purchased 2 months in advance of production. January purchases are intended for use in March production. Since payment is due 2 months after purchase, payment will be made in March. Thus:

Month of:				*Month of:*	
Sale	Production	Um	Ub	Purchase	Payment
February	January	54 000	90 000	November	January
March	February	96 000	160 000	December	February
April	March	108 000	180 000	January	March

4. In addition to the above it is also possible to produce a budgeted balance sheet at the end of the budget period.

5. While it may appear that the operating budgets were compiled before the cash budget, the budgets are really drawn up in conjunction with each other. Notice, for example, that the interest charge in the budgeted income statement could not be determined without knowledge of the cash deficit reflected in the cash budget and giving rise to the interest payment.

6. Due to items such as investments in machinery, debtors and stock, the use of trade finance, and expenses which do not involve the flow of cash, this example clearly illustrates that profit and cash are not necessarily equal.

MOTIVATION AND CONTROL

Earlier in this chapter it was mentioned that budgets may be used as motivating and control tools. To do this effectively, budgets for particular departments should contain only those items that are controllable by those departments. This is because managers can only be held responsible for items under their control. Clearly if this were not the case it is unlikely that the managers would be positively motivated. This concept is known as responsibility accounting.

Closely related to the above is the concept of flexible budgeting. This is of assistance in the control function and may best be illustrated by way of example.

Refer to the example above where variable selling expenses are budgeted at R86 000.

Assume that at the end of the 3 month period, selling expenses amount to R90 000. Can it be said that variable selling expenses have been R4 000 too high?

Consider how the figure of R86 000 was derived. Selling expenses were budgeted at R2 per unit sold, and 43 000 units were expected to be sold. Assume that at the end of the 3 month period 50 000 units were sold. The budget should now be 'flexed' to take this into account i.e. given that 50 000 units were sold, variable expenses are now expected to be R100 000 (50 000 × R2). It can now be said that selling has underspent by R10 000 (R100 000 − R90 000). Note this is not necessarily a good situation, it is a signal for management to investigate the area and establish the cause. This area is examined in the following chapter.

Reference has been made in this chapter to management control systems. Many may argue that they do not have a system or are too small for a system. We suggest that even though some businesses may not have a formalised system of management control, they have some degree of informal system by which some of the principles raised in this chapter are implicitly applied.

QUESTIONS

10.1 Joe Sweet is head of a productive division of the Caramele Company. He is responsible for the performance of his division. Explain why each of the items listed below should or should not fall within his budget.

1. Raw materials
2. Foreman's salary
3. Repairs and maintenance of machinery
4. Repairs and maintenance of factory building
5. Head office charge of R5 000 per month for overheads.
6. Charge for the use of the company computer. The charge is based on the time the computer is utilised by the division.
7. Charge for goods purchased from another division of the same company.

10.2 Maruli started operations at the beginning of January 19X5. Details of its first year of operation follow:

	(000's)
Sales	R2 000
Cost of sales	1 500
Acquisition of plant	500
Depreciation of fixed assets	100
Loans raised	200
Bad debts	30
Other operating expenses	200

Note
— 90% of sales had been collected
— all trade creditors had been paid
— the proprietors introduced R200 000 into the business at the start.

REQUIRED

What is the bank balance at 31 December 19X5?

10.3 The Solex Company plan to sell 10 000 units of finished goods in March and 15 000 in April. Each unit requires:

1 kg of material A
2 kg of material B

Stocks at 1 March are

Finished goods	5 000 units
Material A	2 000 kgs
Material B	3 000 kgs

It is the policy of Solex to have enough stock on hand at the end of a month to supply 50% of the following month's sales.

REQUIRED

Calculate the raw materials to be purchased during March assuming the company wishes to maintain the same relationship between raw material and finished goods stock as is currently the case.

10.4 Poppee Ltd, a widely diversified company, intends manufacturing skicaps for the first time in the new season.

The following information is available.

Selling price: R10 per unit for cash
               R11 per unit on 60 days credit

The demand for the product is constant from month to month, and all sales are split evenly between cash and credit sales.

Variable manufacturing costs:

Direct materials	R3,00 per unit
Direct labour	R1,00 per unit
Variable overheads	R1,50 per unit

Variable overheads comprise 50c per unit for indirect labour and R1 per unit for indirect materials.

Poppee obtains 30 days credit from the suppliers of material; all labour costs are paid in the month in which they are incurred.

Fixed costs:

Rent — R2 000 per month payable at the end of each month

Depreciation — R3 000 per annum

Administration — R15 000 per annum made up of:

(i) A salary of R1 000 per month payable to a manager employed to supervise the skicap operation.

(ii) R1 500 general administration expenses allocated by the accounting department every 6 months. The manufacture of skicaps will not increase the administration costs of the company as a whole.

Additional information:

Plant costing R3 000 will be installed on the first day of operation and must be paid for within 90 days.

The skicaps are manufactured under licence which costs R2 000, payable on commencement of operations. A royalty of 50c on each unit sold is payable at the end of the year.

There will be no stocks of finished goods or raw materials on hand at any stage.

REQUIRED

1. Calculate the net cash inflow (or outflow) for the year as a result of the manufacture and sale of skicaps if sales for the first year are 15 000 units.

2. Calculate the number of units to be sold in the first six months of operations so that the manufacture and sale of skicaps results in neither a cash inflow nor cash outflow at the end of the first six months (i.e. calculate the number of units to be sold to achieve a cash breakeven at the end of six months).

11 Standard Costing

Standard costing is a powerful management tool. It can be used to alert management to areas where deviations from expected performance have occurred. Standard costing bridges the planning and control functions of budgeting and the 'hands on' operational control required on the factory floor.

Standard costing is a simple and effective means of exercising control over operations. There are few factories which do not apply standard costing to some degree.

While standard costing has its most frequent application in the control of manufacturing operations, the principles may be applied to the control of any repetitive function within an organisation as well as to non-manufacturing operations.

The following example is intended to illustrate the technique and the principles involved in standard costing. Some further important issues, which are not covered in the example, are discussed at the end of this chapter.

The technique is dependent on the use of flexible budgeting which was introduced in the previous chapter.

Consider the following information:

Budgeted manufacturing cost month 1	R300 000
Actual manufacturing cost month 1	R371 100
Deviation from budget	R 71 100

At first sight one could simply report that there is a deviation of R71 100 from budgeted manufacturing cost. But this would be an over-simplification as it fails to analyse the constituents of the difference. These may include the different costs involved (materials, labour, fixed and variable overheads), and the fact that the budgeted level of activity may differ from the actual level of activity.

This can be illustrated by expanding the above figures to incorporate the composition of the budget and of actual cost.

Level of activity		Budget	Actual	Difference
Units		10 000	11 900	1 900
Hours	3 hours/unit	30 000	35 000	1 500
Material A	R10/unit	100 000	119 000	19 000 (u)
Material B	R10/unit	100 000	132 600	32 600 (u)
Labour	R1/hour	30 000	38 500	8 500 (u)
Variable overhead	R2/hr	60 000	70 000	10 000 (u)
Fixed overhead	R33⅓/hr	10 000	11 000	1 000 (u)
		R300 000	R371 100	R71 100 (u)

u = unfavourable

This table illustrates the differences by item of manufacturing cost and also indicates that there is a difference between budgeted and actual level of activity. This means that we should not make a direct comparison between the actual and budgeted information. We should rather ask: what would the budgeted cost have been if we had known what the actual level of activity was going to be, and had budgeted for that level?

The use of a flexible budget assists in making a valid analysis. Therefore the above table will be restated and a flexible budget inserted. A flexible budget is compiled using the budgeted rates for the actual level of activity. For example 11 900 units should take 35 700 hours [11 900 × 3] and variable overhead should be R71 400 [35 700 × 2].

	Budget	Flexible Budget	Actual	Difference
Units	10 000	11 900	11 900	nil
Hours 3 hours/unit	30 000	35 700	35 000	700 (f)
Material A R10/unit	100 000	119 000	119 000	nil
Material B R10/unit	100 000	119 000	132 600	13 600 (u)
Labour R1/hour	30 000	35 700	38 500	2 800 (u)
Variable overheads R2/hour	60 000	71 400	70 000	1 400 (f)
Fixed overheads R33⅓/hour	10 000	11 900	11 000	900 (f)
	R300 000	R357 000	R371 100	R14 100 (u)

u = unfavourable
f = favourable

The difference between budgeted and actual cost may now be analysed.

It can now be said that the difference between budgeted and actual cost has arisen as follows:

As a result of increased level of activity	57 000
[357 000 − 300 000]	
As a result of deviations in various cost items	14 100
Total difference between budget and actual	R71 100
[371 100 − 300 000]	

The difference between the flexible budget and the actual costs, in this case R14 100, will be the subject of detailed variance analysis. Variance analysis identifies the specific areas where the differences arose (for example material price, material usage) and highlights areas requiring further investigation.

We will now proceed to analyse the variances based on the previous table and on the following information.

A factory produces 2 articles, X and Y:

Standard cost of one unit of X is:

Material A—10 kg @ R1/kg	R10
Material B—1 kg @ R10/kg	10
Labour—3 hours @ R1/hr	3
Variable overhead—200% of standard labour cost	6
Fixed overhead—3 hours @ 33⅓c per hour	1

Budgeted production 10 000 units per month
Fixed costs R120 000 per annum

For a particular month the actual production and related costs for X were as follows:

Units produced	11 900 units
Material A	119 000 kg @ R1
Material B	13 000 kg @ R10,20
Labour	35 000 hrs @ R1,10
Variable overhead	R70 000
Fixed overhead	R11 000

The following variances may now be calculated:

Material variances

Material price variance

This indicates by how much the cost of the materials used differs from the standard cost

Material A:
Standard cost R1/kg
Actual cost   R1/kg
No material price variance

Material B:

Standard cost R10,00/kg
Actual cost   R10,20/kg
Material price variance R0,20/kg (u)
  [Material B cost 20c per kg more than expected]
Used 13 000 kg
Total material price variance for the month
  R26 000 (u) [13 000 × 0,20]
  [13 000 kg of material were used each costing
  20c extra]

Possible causes of a material price variance include:

— the price may have gone up
— better prices negotiated
— quantity discount
— different quality
— different suppliers
— standards incorrectly set or need revision.

Another issue to be considered is the point at which material price variances are extracted. If stock records are maintained at standard prices, then when goods are purchased the price variance is determined and isolated, and the goods are recorded in the stock records at standard price and eventually issued to production at standard price. On the other hand the goods may be recorded in the stock records at actual price. Only when the goods are eventually issued to production will the price variance be extracted.

Either method is acceptable. The former assumes the purchasing and the production functions to be totally divorced while the latter views purchasing as a factor of production. The authors prefer the former since this permits the disclosure of variances at an earlier stage, enabling any action that may need to be taken to be more effective.

Material usage variance

This indicates the cost of using an amount of material different from the standard usage

Material A:

Standard usage 10 kg per unit	
Actual usage for 11 900 units	119 000 kg
Budgeted usage for 11 900 units	119 000 kg
Difference	nil

∴ No material usage variance

Material B:

Standard usage 1 kg per unit

Actual usage for 11 900 units	13 000 kg
Budgeted usage for 11 900 units	11 900 kg
Difference	1 100 kg (u)

∴ Material usage variance 1 100 × R10 = R11 000 (u)

(Note that the material usage variance is measured at standard cost as the price variance has already been calculated and eliminated.)

Possible causes of a material usage variance include:

— accidental wastage
— labour efficiency
— management supervision
— different quality
— standards incorrectly set or need revision.

Summary	Price Variance	Usage Variance	Total
Material A	nil	nil	nil
Material B	2 600 (u)	11 000 (u)	13 600 (u)
	R2 600 (u)	R11 000 (u)	R13 600 (u)

Notice that the variance for each material agrees with the total as calculated on the table presented earlier.

The usage variance may be analysed further into a mix and yield variance. These variances will only be calculated in cases where a mixing process is involved, for example, in the paint industry. This is not applicable in cases where component parts are involved.

Assuming that we are dealing with a mixing process, the mix and yield variances will be calculated as follows:

	A		B		TOTAL	
	kg	R	kg	R	kg	R
Standard mix for actual input at standard price (note 1)	120 000	120 000	12 000	120 000	132 000	240 000
Actual mix at standard price	119 000	119 000	13 000	130 000	132 000	249 000
MIX VARIANCE (Note 2)						R9 000 (u)

	A kg	R	B kg	R	TOTAL kg	R
Standard mix for actual output at standard price	119 000	119 000	11 900	119 000	130 900	238 000
Standard mix for actual input at standard price	120 000	120 000	12 000	120 000	132 000	240 000
YIELD VARIANCE (Note 2)						R2 000 (u)

Check:			
Usage variance A			nil
Usage variance B			11 000 (u)
			R11 000 (u)
Mix variance			9 000 (u)
Yield variance			2 000 (u)
			R11 000 (u)

Alternative calculation for yield variance

For actual input of 132 000 kg:

Expected output of $\dfrac{132\,000}{11}$ i.e.	12 000 units
Actual yield	11 900 units
Shortfall in yield	100 units
i.e. A [100 units $\times$ 10 kg $\times$ R1]	1 000
B [100 units $\times$ 1 kg $\times$ R10]	1 000
	R2 000

Notes:

1. Total input was 132 000 kg. Standard input for 1 unit is 10 kg of A and 1 kg of B

   i.e. Ratio of A:B is 10:1

   i.e. Standard mix for 132 000 kg would be

   $$\frac{132\,000}{1} \times \frac{10}{11} = 120\,000 \text{ kg A}$$

   $$\frac{132\,000}{1} \times \frac{1}{11} = 12\,000 \text{ kg B}$$

2. To calculate individual mix or yield variances for A and B would be meaningless as the variance arises as a result of the total mixture varying. The individual amounts are irrelevant, it is the *total* which is of concern.

Labour variances

Labour rate variance

This indicates by how much the actual rate of pay has deviated from the standard rate. The calculation is similar to the material price variance.

Standard rate of pay   R1,00/hr
Actual rate of pay   R1,10/hr
Difference   R0,10/hr (u)

Number of hours paid for—35 000 hrs
∴ labour rate variance R3 500 (u) [35 000 × 0,10]

Possible causes of labour rate variances include:
- changes in rate of pay
- different grade of labour
- overtime
- standards incorrectly set or need revision.

Labour efficiency variance

This indicates the effect of deviation from standard time allowed for production. The calculation is similar to the material usage variance. The variance may also be analysed further into labour mix and a true labour efficiency variance in cases where there are different grades of labour.

Standard time for production   35 700 hours
Actual time taken   35 000 hours
Difference   700 hours (f)

Standard cost per hour R1

labour efficiency variance R700 (f) [700 × 1]

Note that the efficiency variance plus the rate variance [R700 (f) + R3 500 (u)] is equal to the total variance of R2 800 (u) per the table.

Possible causes of labour efficiency variances include:
- different grade of labour
- quality of materials
- supervision
- motivation of workforce
- standards incorrectly set or need revision.

Variable overhead variances

Variable overhead rate variance

This indicates by how much the variable overhead incurred has differed from the expected rate of incurrence.

Standard rate of incurrence   R2/hr
Actual rate of incurrence   R2/hr [70 000 ÷ 35 000]
Difference   NIL

Therefore no variable overhead rate variance has occurred.

Possible causes of variable overhead rate variances include:
— poor controls
— price changes
— mismatch between basis of accounting for overheads and actually incurring overheads
— standards incorrectly set or need revision.

Variable overhead efficiency variance

This indicates the effect of deviation from standard time allowed for actual production.

Standard time for production	35 700 hours
Actual time taken	35 000 hours
Difference	700 hours (f)

Standard rate per hour R2

∴ variable overhead efficiency variance R1 400 (f) [700 × 2]

Note that the efficiency variance plus the rate variance [1 400 (f) + NIL] is equal to the total variance of R1 400 (f) per the table.

The reasons for variable overhead efficiency variances are related to the basis on which they are absorbed, in this case labour hours.

Fixed overhead variances

In the case of the variances discussed previously the difference between the actual figures and the flexible budget were considered.

In the case of the fixed overheads the total variance to be considered is also the difference between the flexible budget and the actual amount spent. However this is caused by the interaction of two quite separate phenomena, expenditure and the absorption rate.

Fixed overhead spending variance

This indicates the difference between budgeted expenditure and actual expenditure.

Budgeted fixed overheads	R10 000
Actual fixed overheads	R11 000
Fixed overhead spending variance	R1 000 (u)

Possible causes of fixed overhead spending variances include:
— price changes
— control over expenditure
— unscheduled expenditure
— budget needs revision.

Fixed overhead volume variance

This indicates the difference between budgeted absorption and the amount actually absorbed.

Fixed overhead absorbed	
[35 700 × 0,33⅓]	R11 900
Budgeted absorption	10 000
Fixed overhead volume variance	R1 900 (f)

The fixed overhead absorption rate was budgeted at 33⅓ cents per hour.

The budgeted hours of production	
amounted to	30 000 hours
Actual hours of production	
amounted to	35 700 standard hours
Extra hours of production	5 700 hours

Thus overheads were absorbed over an additional 5 700 hours. In monetary terms this amounts to 5 700 × 33⅓ cents = R1 900

Note that the spending variance and the volume variance [R1 000 (u) plus R1 900 (f)] is equal to the total variance of R900 (f) per the table.

The fixed overhead volume variance may be further analysed into an efficiency variance and a capacity variance.

However the fixed overhead variance arises solely as a consequence of the activity level differing from that budgeted for, therefore calculating these variances provides management with no additional information. In fact modern thinking is that these variances should not be calculated as they can be misleading.

If direct costing were used instead of absorption costing then the only fixed overhead variance would be the spending variance. This is because the spending variance is the only fixed overhead variance that emanates from a difference in the cost of fixed overheads. All the other fixed overhead variances emanate from deviation in the absorption. Since direct costing ignores the absorption of overheads there can be no variances as a result of under or over absorption.

Sales variances

Variances resulting from deviations from budgeted sales may also be analysed in a similar manner to the variances previously discussed.

Extending the above example:

In addition, you are aware that for this particular month the following information relates to sales of X and Y.

Budgeted sales   X 10 000 units at R40
                        Y 20 000 units at R50
Actual sales   X 11 900 units at R38
                        Y 15 000 units at R50

Standard variable costs of producing Y are R40/unit and the actual costs for the month were R600 000.

Fixed costs for article Y are budgeted to be R180 000 p.a. and the actual cost was R15 000 for the month. Fixed costs are accounted for on a direct costing basis.

A table comparing the budget, the flexible budget and the actual performance may be constructed.

	Budget	Flexible Budget	Actual	Difference
Units X	10 000	11 900	11 900	
Y	20 000	15 000	15 000	
Sales X R40/unit	400 000	476 000	452 200	23 800 (u)
Y R50/unit	1 000 000	750 000	750 000	—
Total sales	R1 400 000	R1 226 000	R1 202 200	R23 800 (u)
Variable cost X R29/unit	290 000	345 100	360 100	15 000 (u)
Y R40/unit	800 000	600 000	600 000	—
Total variable costs	R1 090 000	R945 100	R960 100	R15 000 (u)
Contribution	R310 000	R280 900	R242 100	R38 800 (u)
Fixed costs X	10 000	10 000	11 000	1 000 (u)
Y	15 000	15 000	15 000	—
Total fixed costs	R25 000	R25 000	R26 000	R1 000 (u)
Profit	R285 000	R255 900	R216 100	R39 800 (u)

Deviation from expected expenditure has already been analysed; it now remains to analyse the effect of deviation from planned sales.

Sales price variance

Product X   Actual selling price   R38 per unit
                Budgeted selling price   R40 per unit
                Difference   R 2 (u)

Sales price variance   R2 (u) × 11 900 = R23 800 (u)

Product Y   Actual selling price   R50 per unit
                Budgeted selling price   R50 per unit
                Difference   Nil

No sales price variance

Note that these amounts are in agreement with those reflected in the above table.

Possible causes of sales price variances include:
— increased prices
— volume discounts
— special offers
— standards incorrectly set or need revision.

At this stage the difference between actual performance and the flexible budget has been analysed. Given a certain level of activity management has been able to isolate the difference in the results, investigate them and take such action as may be considered necessary.

However the differences between the actual results and the budgeted results have not yet been analysed. They may be due partly to variation in prices, usage, etc. as analysed above, and partly to the deviation from budgeted activity. The deviation from budgeted activity will now be analysed.

Sales mix variance

This variance, also known as the contribution mix variance, measures the effect of changes in the sales mix given a level of sales.

	X	Y
Actual sales	11 900	15 000
Actual sales in budgeted mix (1:2)	8 967	17 933
Difference (units)	2 933 (f)	2 933 (u)
Standard contribution	11 [40 − 29]	10 [50 − 40]
	32 263 (f)	29 330 (u)

Sales mix variance R2 933 (f) [32 263 (f) + 29 330 (u)]

The mix variance only has significance as a total i.e. it may be said that due to a change in the sales mix R2 933 was gained. The figures relating individually to X and Y of R32 263 (f) and R29 330 (u) respectively are meaningless in themselves.

Sales volume variances

This measures the effect of deviations in the quantity sold.

	X	Y	Total
Budgeted sales units	10 000	20 000	30 000
Actual sales in budgeted mix (1:2)	8 967	17 933	26 900
Difference (units)	1 033 (u)	2 067 (u)	3 100 (u)
Standard contribution per unit	11	10	
Sales volume variance	R11 363 (u)	R20 670 (u)	R32 033 (u)

Note that the sales mix variance and the sales volume variance account for the difference between the profits reflected in the budget and the flexible budget.

Budget	285 000
Flexible budget	255 900
Difference	R29 100 (u)
Sales mix variance	2 933 (f)
Sales volume variance	32 033 (u)
	R29 100 (u)

Most businesses have a wide range of products, and it is therefore often impractical to determine the volume and mix variances by considering variations in the units sold. An alternative is to analyse these variances in terms of the differences in the money value of sales.

Sales mix variance

Standard contribution in relation to sales value [310 000 ÷ 1 400 000]	
Standard contribution at actual level of sales (per flexible budget)	R280 900
Had sales been in standard mix contribution would have been [1 226 000 × 310 000 ÷ 1 400 000]	271 471
∴ Sales mix variance	R9 429 (f)

Sales volume variance

Budgeted sales	1 400 000
Actual sales at standard prices	1 226 000
Difference	R174 000 (u)
Loss of contribution resulting from drop in sales volume [174 000 × 310 000 ÷ 1 400 000]	R38 529 (u)

Sales mix variance	R9 429 (f)
Sales volume variance	38 529 (u)
	R29 100 (u)

Note that the mix and volume variances generated by using this method are not the same as those under the unit method. This is because the mix and volume are analysed in terms of different criteria. However, the total of the two will always be the same.

Possible causes of sales mix and quantity variances include:

— price changes
— marketing effort
— efficiency of sales force
— special promotions
— standards incorrectly set or need revision.

Reconciliation

The variance analysis should be presented in a report form to management. As with all reports it should be organised in a logical and easily understandable manner. For example variances pertaining to similar matters should be lumped together, so that the net effect is clearly visible. The report should reconcile the budgeted profit with the actual profit, showing the standard profit in the body.

An example of what a variance report could look like for the above data is as follows:

Trading account for the month

Budgeted profit		R285 000
Sales variances		
mix	9 429 (f)	
volume	38 529 (u)	29 100 (u)
Standard profit		255 900
Expenditure variances		
Materials		
B price	2 600 (u)	
mix	9 000 (u)	
yield	2 000 (u)	13 600 (u)
Labour		
rate	3 500 (u)	
efficiency	700 (f)	2 800 (u)

Variable overheads efficiency	1 400 (f)	
Fixed overheads spending	1 000 (u)	
	16 000 (u)	
Sales variances X-price	23 800 (u)	39 800 (u)
Actual profit		R216 100

The variances detailed are not exhaustive, these are merely some of the more common ones. Variances may be extracted for any occurrence and to whatever degree of detail considered to be useful. For example, senior management may only be interested in the fact that the total profit for the above factory showed an unfavourable variance of R68 900. The factory foreman, on the other hand, will certainly be interested in the fact that labour showed an efficiency variance of 700 hours.

The importance of variance analysis is that it produces a signal for further investigation. In this regard care must be taken not to ignore small variances too readily as they may result from compensating factors. Similarly, it would be naïve to assume favourable variances to be good and unfavourable to be bad. For example, a material price variance is R1 000 (f). On investigation it may be found that inferior quality goods were purchased and material usage reflected an unfavourable variance of R1 500 as a result of these inferior materials.

In analysing variances consideration should be given to the setting of the standards. Unattainable or too loose standards may result in variances which highlight unrealistic standard setting rather than areas requiring management attention. Moreover there are important motivating consequences of setting standards without due care.

QUESTIONS

11.1 Hurt Ltd uses a standard costing system. Details for the production in April are as follows:

Budgeted production	2 000 units
Actual production	1 900 units
Raw material used	3 900 kg
Labour applied	10 000 hours
Raw material cost	R8 300
Labour paid	R48 000
Fixed overhead	R25 000

The standard cost of producing 1 unit is

Raw material 2 kg	R4
Labour 5 hours	R25
Variable costs of 1 unit	R29

Budgeted fixed overhead R20 000

REQUIRED

Calculate all variances using a variable costing system.

11.2 Refer to the data in question 11.1.

REQUIRED

Calculate the overhead variances using a full costing system.

11.3 Guido Pincini uses a standard costing system for the control of his pizzeria. Each batch of 10 pizzas require:

4 kg ripe tomatoes @	R1,00 per kg.
3 kg sweet onions @	R0,50 per kg.
6 kg mozarella cheese @	R5,00 per kg.

One day the cheese failed to arrive on time and Guido feared the cheese on hand would not last the evening. Rather than contaminate his pizza with any other cheese Guido decided to be a little less generous with the cheese and fill the pizza with more of the other ingredients.

That evening Guido made 200 pizzas and used

83 kg ripe tomatoes which cost him	R90
66 kg of onions at a cost of	R30
100 kg of cheese costing	R500

REQUIRED

Calculate all variances.

11.4 Sflufk Ltd uses a direct standard costing system in the manufacture and sale of Dats. The applicable standards are:

Selling price		R10
Materials 2 kg @ R1	2	
Manufacturing labour and variable overhead 2 hrs @ R3	6	8
Standard contribution		R2

The factory operates at full capacity and sells all its production (1 000 Dats monthly). No stocks are kept.

During the month of June the following details applied:

Sales 1 100 units	R10 600
Materials 2 500 kg	R1 750
Labour and variable overheads 2 250 hours	R8 000

The company had agreed to repurchase 100 Dats from a customer who could not use them. These units were repurchased at R4 each and sold to a jobber for R700.

Sflufk rewards the managers of the manufacturing and buying divisions by paying them a bonus of 10% of the net favourable variances which arose in their respective sections. If there are net unfavourable variances they are carried forward until they may be set off against favourable variances.

REQUIRED

(a) Calculate all variances for the month June.
(b) State with suitable explanations which variances may have resulted from the bonus scheme in operation.
(c) Comment on the weaknesses of the bonus scheme.
(d) Suggest one measure which will overcome the weaknesses identified in *(c)*.

11.5 A company has a production capacity of 12 500 units per month. Sales are normally only 10 000 units per month. At normal capacity overheads total R35 000, or R3,50 per unit.

During January 12 000 units were manufactured and sold, and overheads amounted to R39 000 or R3,25 per unit.

An argument has arisen between the plant manager and the foreman. The foreman claims that he should be given credit for cutting the unit cost by 25 cents. The manager believes that waste and inefficiency have been experienced in the plant. He insists that the foreman has allowed costs to increase in spite of the decrease in unit cost.

The managing director of the company cannot understand the manager's argument and has consulted you in this matter.

Your investigation reveals fixed overheads to be R20 000 per month.

REQUIRED

Prepare a report for the managing director, clarifying the points raised by both parties.

12 Stock Control

For many businesses stock constitutes one of the major assets and must therefore be carefully controlled. Control of stock implies both the quality and the quantity; it is the latter aspect which is the subject of this chapter.

Small businesses often maintain no stock records and merely carry out a periodic physical stock count. This provides very little control over stock other than through monitoring gross profit percentages. It is far better for a business to maintain perpetual stock records. This amounts to simply keeping a stock card for each type of stock much in the same manner as maintaining debtors or creditors accounts. Periodic physical checks should then be carried out and the physical count compared to the stock records. Discrepancies are consequently highlighted, enabling corrective action to be taken.

STOCK COSTS

The greater the quantity of stock that is held, the greater will be the expense that is incurred. This expense will include the cost of financing and storing the stock holding. On the other hand, holding insufficient stock could also result in cost to the business. This cost may take the form of loss of sales resulting in loss of customer goodwill, or additional costs in procuring the stock item outside of normal channels.

Each time stock is ordered, costs associated with ordering arise. On the other hand, the cost of holding stock increases with the length of time for which the stock is held. The cost of holding stock may be diagrammatically represented as follows:

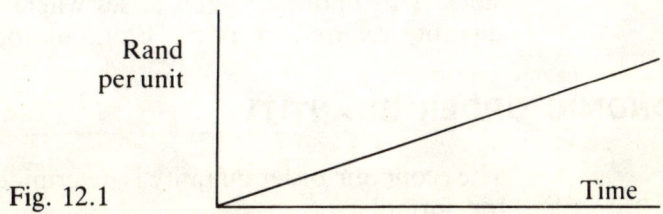

Fig. 12.1

Figure 12.1 illustrates that the longer the stock is held, the greater will be the cost.

The cost of ordering stock may be diagrammatically represented as follows:

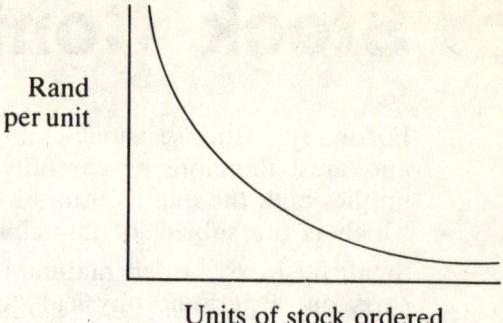

Fig 12.2

Figure 12.2 illustrates that the greater the quantity of stock ordered the lower the cost of ordering per unit.

If the above graphs are superimposed, they would appear as follows:

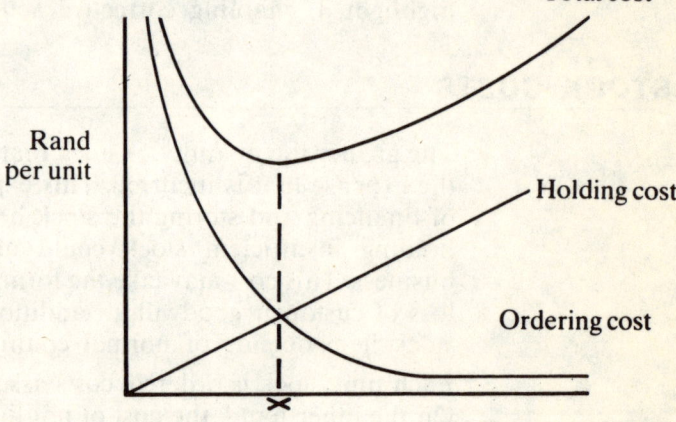

Fig. 12.3   Stock (units)

Figure 12.3 illustrates that the lowest total cost arises when the cost of holding the stock is equal to the cost of ordering the stock. This optimum point arises where orders are placed in a quantity referred to as the economic order quantity (EOQ).

ECONOMIC ORDER QUANTITY

The economic order quantity is determined by using the following formula:

$$E = \sqrt{\frac{2AP}{S}}$$

where E = the economic order quantity
       A = the annual consumption of the stock item
       P = the total costs of placing each order
       S = the cost of holding one item in stock for one year

For example: Given that the annual consumption of a stock item is 10 000 units, each time an order is placed it costs R16 and the cost of holding one item in stock for one year is R8. We can determine the economic order quantity by applying the formula as follows:

$$E = \sqrt{\frac{2AP}{S}}$$

$$= \sqrt{\frac{2 \times 10\,000 \times 16}{8}}$$

$$= 200 \text{ units}$$

This can be checked to see whether it is in fact the order quantity at which the cost of holding and ordering the stock will be equal to each other.

The cost of holding the stock will be the average number of units held multiplied by the cost of holding each item. As orders are made in multiples of 200 units there will be an average of 100 units of stock held, so the total cost of holding the stock will be R800 [100 × R8]. Since 10 000 units are consumed annually and the orders are for 200 units this means that 50 $\left[\dfrac{10\,000}{200}\right]$ orders will be placed annually, the annual cost of ordering would be R800 [50 × R16].

The total cost of holding an average stock of these 100 units is therefore R1 600 based on an economic order quantity of 200 units.

Had the decision been to order in quantities of 1 000 units the total cost would be:

Holding cost: average stock of 500 units

$\left[\dfrac{1\,000}{2}\right]$ at R8 per unit   4 000

Ordering costs: 10 $\left[\dfrac{10\,000}{100}\right]$ orders at R16 per order   160

Total cost of a 1 000 unit order quantity   R4 160

This may be contrasted to the cost determined using the EOQ.

Graphically illustrated, the consumption pattern of stock would be as follows:

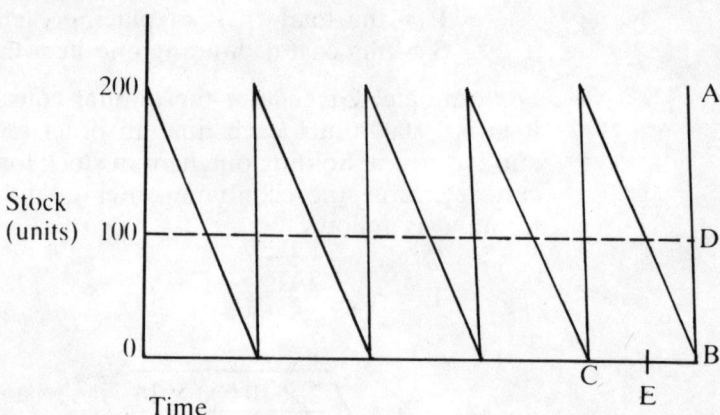

A–B represents the economic order quantity
C–B represents the time of consumption of the stock holding
B–D represents the average stock holding
E–B represents lead time (see following)

LEAD TIME BUFFER STOCK AND RE-ORDER POINT

An important factor in stock control is the determination of lead time, which refers to the time lag between placing an order and receipt of the goods. Lead time is critical in determining when to re-order so as to avoid carrying too much stock or being out of stock.

Referring back to the example, if we assume that the business works a 50-week year, this means that weekly consumption is 200 units $\left[\dfrac{10\,000}{50}\right]$. If we then calculate that daily usage is 40 units $\left[\dfrac{200\text{ units}}{5\text{ days}}\right]$ and that the lead time is 3 days [E–B], this means that when stock is drawn down to a level of 120 units [3 × 40] an order must be placed to ensure that the optimum is achieved.

However, as we are dealing with average consumption figures, it is unlikely that 40 units will be consumed each and every day. To take this into account many businesses hold stock in excess of their normal expected requirements. This excess stock is referred to as buffer stock.

The decision as to the amount of buffer stock to hold, if any, will depend upon the cost of holding the buffer stock as opposed to the cost of being out of stock. In our example each additional unit held as buffer stock will cost R8 per annum. Assuming an economic order quantity of 200 units and a buffer stock of 25 units, the annual cost of holding buffer stock will add R200 [25 × R8] to the previously determined cost of R1 600 associated with the EOQ of 200 units.

In deciding on the level of buffer stock to hold, the R200 cost of holding buffer stock must be weighed up against the cost of being out of stock.

Once re-order levels have been determined based on order quantities and lead times, various methods may be employed to signal that the re-order level has been reached. An example is the use of a bin system where the staff are instructed to generate an order when the first item is taken out of a specially marked container.

MATERIALITY

Materiality is always a consideration in deciding on the extent of control to be exercised. A generalisation is that 20% of stock by volume accounts for 80% of stock by value. Clearly, it is towards this 20% holding that most of management's attention should be directed. As regards the balance of the stock it may be adequate to decide intuitively on order quantities and re-order levels if the amount involved is immaterial.

A simple yet useful management practice is to apply the ABC method of stock classification. This entails simply classifying stock into various categories and applying such control measures over each category as is deemed appropriate. In this way strict control and/or sophisticated ordering methods may be applied to only a small quantity of stock which comprises most of the value of the total stockholding. Occasional random checks may be applied to control the low value stock.

QUESTIONS

12.1 Explain how Pareto's Law (the 80:20 principle) may be applied to stock control.

12.2 What must be estimated to calculate the economic order quantity? How reliable would your estimates be? Why?

12.3 The following annual costs refer to the stock of a company which buys and sells a product:

Cost of item	R2,00
Transport in	0,20
Storage	0,20
Insurance	0,05
Selling price	5,00
Transport out	0,15
Selling expenses	0,25

The company buys 20 000 units each year and the opportunity cost of the funds invested is R2 500.

REQUIRED

Calculate the annual carrying cost per unit.

12.4 Onetimslat Ltd sells play tables which are imported at a cost of R10 from Hong Kong. For some years now the company has been ordering every month to satisfy the annual demand of 1 200 units. It is now proposed that the company should place one order to satisfy the entire year's demand. The reason forwarded is that because the lines of communication between supplier and purchaser are so poor ordering costs are very high at R100 per order, it would therefore be cheaper to place only one order as opposed to twelve. Costs of carrying one play table in stock for a year are 5% of purchase price.

From the time of starting to place an order and receiving the goods a period of 3 months usually elapses, although it is often much more and sometimes less.

The identical tables are available from Sweden, but since they are painted a fabulous yellow they cost 20c per table more than the Hong Kong price. Due to better communication it only costs R12 to place an order and the lead time is one month without fail.

REQUIRED

1. Should the tables be bought from Hong Kong or Sweden if the purchase takes place at the EOQ and the company wishes to minimise costs.

2. How many orders should be placed per year if the tables are bought from the source identified in 1. above. Comment on the company's proposal to place one order per year.

3. The data hints at certain factors which could not be built into your analysis owing to the lack of information. Explain how these and other factors would affect your analysis.

13 Capital Investment Appraisal

A business may embark on several different types of capital investment; these usually fall into one of the following three categories.

1. Replacements—Assets which are currently in use will eventually cease to be efficient and will need to be replaced.

2. Expansion—Expansion may take two forms:

   2.1 Additional capacity—the business may be approaching full capacity and needs to consider the viability of increasing its capacity e.g. by acquiring additional plant, equipment or factory space.

   2.2 New product—the business may consider the development of a new product or range of products, or the acquisition of another business.

3. Forced investment—the business may be forced by statute, or social pressure to invest in projects such as pollution control or improvement of staff facilities.

The need for capital budgeting

Any of the alternatives mentioned above may be major in terms of money, time and resources. Because of their importance it is imperative that they be adequately planned and controlled. Some of the aspects to be considered include:

— the effects and consequences of the projects need to be studied closely, both in the short and in the long term. While a numerical evaluation of the project may indicate a certain course of action, factors such as the affect on staff or other products must be considered, and also whether the business has the expertise to carry out the project;

— the timing of the project needs to be carefully planned and coordinated. It would be absurd to hire the staff now to operate a new plant which is to be installed in a year's time and which produces a product, the market for which will take three years to establish;

— the methods of financing the project need to be planned. It is probable that large amounts of finance will be required and adequate arrangements need to be made. If the company's normal financiers are suddenly presented with a request for a large sum of money there is a greater likelihood of rejection than if they had been approached well in advance with details of the project and the financing required. Furthermore should the finance be refused, alternative sources of finance can be explored or further negotiations can be conducted. By allowing sufficient time, the company can give full consideration to alternative sources and do some "comparison shopping" on their relative costs.

RANKING PROJECTS

Most businesses have several desirable projects and a limit to their available finance. This gives rise to the question of which projects should be proceeded with and which should be rejected. The projects need to be screened for acceptability (i.e. do they meet certain minimum requirements below which the project will not be acceptable). The acceptable projects then need to be ranked in order of preference.

Clearly a method of measuring alternative projects is required as well as a standard against which to measure them. Four measures will be considered:

Accounting rate of return
Payback
Net present value
Internal rate of return

ACCOUNTING RATE OF RETURN (ARR)

The accounting rate of return may be described as the technique of measuring increased profit generated by the increase in investment. This may be expressed as a percentage as follows:

$$ARR = \frac{Incremental\ profit}{Incremental\ investment} \times \frac{100}{1}$$

A new piece of machinery costing R10 000 will save R3 000 per annum for 10 years. Incremental investment is R10 000 and the incremental income is the saving of R3 000 less depreciation of R1 000 [10 000 ÷ 10 years]. For simplicity the effect of taxation has been ignored.

$$ARR = \frac{2\ 000}{10\ 000} \times 100$$

$$= 20\%$$

The specific way in which the ARR is calculated is open to debate and the method has several weaknesses. However if the

ARR is determined in a consistent manner many of the problems will be overcome as the minimum rate required to accept a project will naturally be selected after considering the method by which the rate is to be determined.

The most significant weakness of this method, and one which cannot be readily overcome, is that the ARR ignores the fact that money has a time value.

PAYBACK PERIOD

The payback period measures the length of time it takes for the project to pay for itself i.e. how long does it take before we get our money back.

The payback may be expressed in the form:

$$\frac{\text{Incremental investment}}{\text{Incremental cash flow}}$$

Using the example above this will be: $\frac{10\,000}{3\,000} = 3,33$ years

Note that the incremental cash flow is R3 000 as depreciation does not involve the flow of funds.

The major weakness of the payback method for evaluating projects is that it does not take profitability into account.

Consider another project which has an investment of R10 000 and a cash saving of R6 000 per annum for 2 years.

This project has a payback period of $\frac{10\,000}{6\,000} = 1,66$ years

The payback is twice as rapid as in the first example, however, the project may yield less profit over its total life.

A further weakness of the payback is that as with the accounting rate of return method it also ignores the time value of money.

In view of these limitations why bother with payback at all?

The payback method is valid in two situations. Firstly it is a very useful measure to consider in conjunction with some other measures. Secondly where a project is subject to a high degree of risk, management may be more concerned with the speed with which the investment is recovered than with the overall profitability.

The payback period is a crude measure of risk; if used in this context it is a useful tool.

TIME VALUE OF MONEY

We noted that a major weakness of the ARR and the payback period, is that both measures ignore the time value of money. Before considering those measures that do take into account the time value of money it is important to understand what this concept means.

If you were offered R1 000 today as a gift you would no doubt be delighted. If on the other hand you were offered a gift of R1 000 in one year's time you would be a little less delighted. How much less delighted would you be? This depends on what you would have planned to do with the money over the next year, since the use you would have made of the money determines its time value.

If you planned to put your R1 000 in a sock and hide it under a floor board to be resurrected in a year's time, the money would have no time value. The R1 000 you salvage from the foundations of your abode and the R1 000 which would otherwise have been given to you as a gift one year later would be exactly the same (except for the dust).

If instead you planned to place your money on fixed deposit at 8% pa then the R1 000 you received today will have grown to R1 080 in a year's time. You would be R80 more delighted at receiving the gift today rather than in one year's time.

This does not mean to say that the time value of money is equal to the interest rate. The time value is related to the use to which the money can be put. Suppose you could place the money in an investment which yields a return of 60% pa. At the end of the year your R1 000 will have grown to R1 600. You would be much more delighted, in fact R600 more delighted, than you would be to receive the gift one year later.

This situation may now be stated the other way round. If you were offered a gift of R1 600 in a year's time how much would you be prepared to accept today to be just as happy. This depends on what you can do with the money during the coming year. If you could earn a return of 60% it can be said that you would be happy to accept R1 000 today instead of R1 600 in one year since at the end of the year you will have R1 600 either way.

The amount that will make us just as happy today, instead of some larger amount in the future, is known as the present value. The present value of some future amount can easily be determined by the use of present value tables or a reasonable calculator once the discount rate is known.

The discount rate will be discussed later in this chapter, at this stage it can be equated to the desired rate of return on the money.

The business will determine its required discount rate and the projects may then be evaluated taking into account the time value of money.

NET PRESENT VALUE (NPV)

The net present value technique determines the cash flows (inflows and outflows) of a project and uses the selected discount rate to reduce these to their present values. The sum of the present values of the cash inflows and outflows will result in the net present value, i.e. the entire project is considered in terms of the present value of money today. If the NPV is zero the project is yielding at least the return required. If it is positive it yields in excess of the return required and if the NPV is negative the project does not yield the required return.

For example: A business is considering investing in a machine costing R1 000 which will generate an income of R300 per annum for 5 years. The business requires a return of 12% per annum.

Cash outflow now	− 1 000
Cash inflow 300 p.a. for 5 years	
Present value annuity factor for 5 years @ 12% = 3,6	
3,6 × 300	+ 1 080
	+ 80
Assume the plant has a salvage value of R50 at the end of the project	
Present value factor in 5 years @ 12% = 0,567	
0,567 × 50	+ 28
Net present value	+ R108

This means that the project will yield more than 12% and is therefore acceptable.

INTERNAL RATE OF RETURN (IRR)

This technique discounts all the cash outflows and inflows and determines the rate at which the net present value will be zero.

Cash outflows × (discount factor) = cash inflows × (discount factor).

The discount factor can be determined and the discount rate applicable to this factor determined. However where the cash flows differ from year to year, this is extremely time-consuming and laborious to determine without calculating aids.

The business will have a rate below which projects will be rejected, so having determined the IRR it will be related to the discount rate and the acceptable projects may be ranked in order of preference.

DISCOUNT RATE

The discount rate is referred to by many terms which include screening rate, cut-off and hurdle rate.

The cost of capital may be the starting point from which to determine the discount rate. If the total of all the projects the firm undertakes to do does not yield a return of at least equivalent to the marginal weighted average cost of capital, the value of the business will decline.

The cost of capital may then be adjusted for risk, inflation, type of project or other factors to establish the appropriate discount rate for a particular project.

RANKING PROJECTS

Four methods of ranking projects have been discussed, ARR, Payback, NPV and IRR. These methods can, and often do, result in different rankings. The question arises as to which technique should be preferred.

The accounting rate of return is unsound and should not be used. The use of this technique will certainly result in the wrong decision being taken on some occasions.

The payback as mentioned earlier ignores the profitability of a project but is nevertheless useful in situations where there is a high degree of risk involved. It is also useful to calculate the payback as additional information in considering any project.

The net present value and the internal rate of return are preferable techniques to employ as both incorporate the time value of money and profitability in their analysis.

The NPV is slightly superior to the IRR as the latter technique assumes reinvestment at that rate in perpetuity which is probably an unjustifiable assumption. Because of this the two techniques occasionally result in conflicting rankings. In such a case the ranking shown by the NPV may be preferable.

Despite that, the IRR is more frequently used in practice. This is probably because many businessmen have a "feel" for a rate of return but find the idea of a net present value awkward. An often stated advantage of using the IRR is that the business is spared having to establish a discount rate. A rate is generated by the technique and management can decide on its acceptability. With the NPV a cut-off rate must be determined in advance. While it is true that the IRR calculation generates a rate, the acceptability of this rate should be objectively evaluated against a predetermined cut-off rate.

It must be emphasised that whatever technique is used the result shown is merely the starting point for decision-making. Managers must then consider all other relevant factors before deciding to embark on or reject the project. Most sophisticated businesses use a combination of several techniques to assist in their decisions.

SOURCES OF FINANCE

Having decided to embark on a project it is necessary to raise the finance if it is not already on hand. In any financing decision there are a number of broad principles that must be borne in mind.

Debt/Equity—The business will have an acceptable balance between debt and equity. In raising finance this balance must be considered.

Long/Short Term—In general it may be said that in order to reduce the level of financial risk in a business, short term assets should be financed from short term funds while long term assets should be financed from long term funds.

Cost—Finance should be raised as cheaply as possible. However it must be remembered that the cost of finance in total must be as cheap as possible over the long term. It may be possible to raise certain funds at very reasonable rates which may necessitate the raising of very expensive funds at some future date to redress the balance between debt and equity.

COST OF CAPITAL

The cost of capital is made up for the weighted average cost of the components of capital. Characteristics of the cost of certain categories of capital are:

Debt—Cost of debt is interest, however since interest is tax deductible the cost is the amount paid by the business after taking into account the tax shield effect.

Preference shares—Cost of preference shares is the dividend, with no consequential tax deduction and hence saving.

Equity—Cost of equity is the return the investor expects, this may be expressed as the dividend plus the expected growth and, as with preference dividends, there is no tax advantage to the company paying the dividend.

Retained income—The cost of retained income is similar to the cost of equity.

In determining a discount rate for the evaluating of projects, the *marginal* weighted average cost of capital should be used. This is the cost of replacing the finance, the historical cost of finance is irrelevant.

Illustrative Example

Fancy Ltd is a very profitable company wishing to expand its activities. Three projects are under consideration:

1. In one of the factories, pants are produced. This product has a very stable sales volume, i.e. 15 000 units per annum. On the current level of advertising this volume is expected to be maintained for a very long time. The plant has ample spare capacity. With an aggressive campaign the sales volume can be doubled for a period of three years after which sales will return to their old level.

   Pants sell for R20 a unit and variable costs amount to R15 a unit. Fixed costs are R60 000 per annum (including R10 000 for depreciation).

   The increased activity will reduce variable costs by R1 per unit for the entire output but an additional supervisor will have to be employed at R5 000 per annum. The promotion will cost R160 000 in the first year and R60 000 in each of the two succeeding years. (These are over and above "normal" advertising expenses of R10 000 per annum.)

2. Management think there is a market for a gimmicky product called Smarty. This market is expected to last 3 years and demand is expected to be 150 000 units in the first year, 180 000 in the second and only 30 000 in the third. The Smartys will yield a contribution of R1 per unit. Fixed costs relating to this project will amount to R23 000 per annum (excluding depreciation).

To produce the Smartys a machine will have to be purchased for R150 000. The machine will be placed in a vacant section of the Pants factory and a rental charge of R3 000 per annum will be allocated to it. This allocation is included in the fixed costs above. The machine attracts investment and initial allowances of 30% and 25% respectively, whereby these percentages of the cost of the machinery are allowed as tax deductions in the year the machinery is brought into use. In addition a wear and tear allowance of $33\frac{1}{3}$% per annum calculated on the cost less the initial allowance, and ignoring any scrap value, is allowed on a straight line basis.

3. A section of one of the service departments now operating on a manual basis can be fully automated by the purchase of a machine for R240 000. This will enable Fancy to get rid of the entire work force of 200 men in the section, earning an average of R2 500 p.a. each. One highly skilled operator will have to be employed at a salary of R20 000 p.a. The net increase in the other fixed costs (including depreciation of R80 000 p.a.) will amount to R130 000 p.a.

The machine does not qualify for capital allowances. Wear and tear at a rate of $33\frac{1}{3}$% per annum will be allowed for tax purposes. The machine will have no value at the end of its 3 year life.

The company pays tax at a rate of 40%.

The company requires an after-tax rate of return of 24% on projects involving the purchase of machinery and of 20% on other projects.

Assume:

1. All cash flows from operations occur at the end of the year.
2. Tax is paid at the end of the year in which it is incurred.

From the above:

1. Advise management regarding these projects based on the net present value of each project.
2. Calculate the payback period on Project 2.
3. Calculate the Internal Rate of Return on Project 3.

The present value of R1 at	20%	24%
in 1 year is	0,833	0,807
2 years is	0,694	0,650
3 years is	0,579	0,525
4 years is	0,482	0,423
5 years is	0,402	0,341

The present value of R1 at	20%	24%
for 1 year is	0,833	0,807
2 years is	1,527	1,457
3 years is	2,106	1,982
4 years is	2,588	2,405
5 years is	2,990	2,746

PROJECT 1

Note	Year				20%	NPV
1	1	Promotion [0,6 × 160 000]			0,833	− 79 968
	2	Promotion [0,6 × 60 000]			0,694	− 24 984
	3	Promotion [0,6 × 60 000]			0,579	− 20 844
	1-3	Sales [15 000 × 6]	90 000			
		Variable cost saved				
		[15 000 × 1]	15 000			
			105 000			
		Supervisor	5 000			
			100 000			
		Tax	40 000			
			60 000	2,107	+ 126 420	
					+ 624	

PROJECT 2

Note	Year			24%	NPV
	0	Machine 150 000		1,000	− 150 000
2	1	Tax shield [0,4 × 0,55 × 150 000]			
		= 33 000		0,807	+ 26 631
1	1	Sales [(150 000 − 20 000) × 0,6]		0,807	+ 62 946
	2	Sales [(180 000 − 20 000) × 0,6]		0,650	+ 62 400
	3	Sales [(30 000 − 20 000) × 0,6]		0,525	+ 3 150
2	1-3	W & T Tax shield 0,4 × 37 500		1,982	+ 29 730
3	3	Scrap value [0,6 × 1 000]		0,525	+ 315
					+ 35 172

PROJECT 3

Year			24%	NPV
0	Machine 240 000		1,000	− 240 000
1-3	Savings [200 × 2 500]	500 000		
	Operator	(20 000)		
	Fixed costs	(50 000)		
		430 000		

Tax

Incremental profit 430 000

less: Wear and Tear 80 000

$$350\,000 \times 40\% \quad \underline{140\,000}$$

$$290\,000 \quad 1,982 + \underline{574\,780}$$

$$+ \underline{334\,780}$$

Therefore all projects are acceptable on an NPV basis.

2. Payback — Project 2

Investment		150 000
Year 1 — Tax shield	33 000	
Cash inflow from trading	78 000	
Tax shield wear and tear	15 000	126 000
Unrecouped investment at end of year 1		24 000

Year 2 — Cash inflow from trading R160 000

$$24 \div 160 \times 12 = 1,8 \text{ months}$$

payback ± 1 year 2 months

3. IRR — Project 3

240 000 = 290 000 (Factor of an annuity for 3 years)

$$240 \div 290 = 0,828 = \text{Factor}$$

This works out to be 107%.

Notes to the solution:

1. Due to the tax deduction only 60% of the expense is treated as a cash flow. Similarly in the case of income only 60% can be considered as flowing through to the business.

2. While the tax allowances in respect of the machinery do not in themselves involve a flow of funds they have the effect of shielding the business from having to pay tax at, in this case, 40% of the amount allowed for tax.

3. As the machine is written down to nil for tax purposes any recoupment up to the original cost will be subject to tax.

QUESTIONS

13.1 List advantages and disadvantages for each of the following measures of investment.
   1. Accounting rate of return
   2. Pay back period
   3. Net present value

13.2 You have R10 000 at your disposal and the following investment opportunities present themselves.

1. Lend R10 000 to your uncle's business and he will give you interest of 25% per annum for 4 years at the end of which he will repay your money.

2. Buy a packaging machine for R10 000. The machine has a life of 4 years and generates a profit of R4 000 each year. After 2 years the machine will need an overhaul costing R3 000 and at the end of its useful life can be sold as scrap metal for R1 000. The tax authorities will permit a wear and tear allowance of 25% per annum straight line.

REQUIRED

Which investment should you choose. You usually invested your money in the bank at 20% interest. You are fairly well off and attract tax at a marginal rate of 50%.

13.3 Alpha Ltd is a successful company in the electronics field. The management of Alpha is keen to expand and is constantly on the lookout for suitable investment opportunities. At the moment Alpha has R1 million available for investment and the following projects are available:

1. A machine to be used in the manufacture of touch sensitive switches. The machine will cost R200 000, it will qualify for investment and initial allowances of 30% and 25% respectively and wear and tear will be allowed on a straight line basis over its useful life, which is expected to be 5 years. The machine is likely to be worthless after 5 years. Five million switches are expected to be required every year. Switches cost 10 cents each from the usual supplier. Alpha expects to manufacture at 9 cents each including depreciation.

2. A company making circuit boards for computerised industrial knitting machines. The shares in the company can be purchased for R500 000. The company is expected to generate an after tax cash profit of R103 000 p.a. The company is expected to be able to operate at this level for the foreseeable future.

3. The chairman has a good friend who wants to get out of his frozen food packaging business. In the words of the friend, "I don't have the financial muscle to make a good go of it nor withstand any setbacks". The business would cost R350 000 and a further R50 000 would be

required almost immediately to boost stocks to a satisfactory level. The level of stock is expected to be R160 000 and R80 000 at the end of years 1 and 2 respectively. The business has no fixed assets and all the packing is done by hand. The purchase price was agreed upon on the following basis:

Stocks	R190 000
Goodwill	R160 000
	R350 000

The friend expects that this business will be run down to nothing evenly over a period of 3 years by which time the packaging industry will be automated, and very probably lucrative. He expects after tax profits to be R165 000 in the first year, R110 000 in the second year and R55 000 in the third year. All transactions are for cash.

4. At a cost of R160 000 Alpha can purchase accommodation for 200 of their own factory workers and their families. A nominal rent of R360 per family would be charged annually. These dwellings are not in very good condition and will require repairs of R2 000 every year. After seven years the accommodation will probably be demolished and the land sold realising a net R10 000. The building attracts no tax allowances whatsoever.

You may assume:
A tax rate of 40%
A desired rate of return of 20%

REQUIRED

1. Calculate the net present value of each project.
2. Calculate the pay back period for each project.

13.4 Refer to the data in 13.3 above and to your solutions to the questions therein.

REQUIRED

Prepare a report recommending which of the projects detailed should be proceeded with. Include in your report an analysis of each project incorporating both qualitative and quantitative considerations.

13.5 The Mackee Company produces farm implements at its factory near Cape Town. The implements are transported to its warehouse in Ermelo, 2 500 km away, by rail at a rate of 50 cents per kg of implements.

The management of Mackee is presently considering whether to purchase a truck for transporting the implements. The following details relate to the truck:

Purchase price	R125 000
Useful life	5 years
Salvage value after 5 years	R25 000
Capacity	10 000 kg
Cash cost of operation	R2 per km

The managing director was initially sceptical as he thought the truck would be unlikely to be a paying proposition if it were to do the Ermelo-Cape Town trip empty. The accountant, however, has negotiated with another company, Camk Ltd, to transport Camk's products from Ermelo to Cape Town on every return trip from the warehouse at a price of R6 000 per load.

Mackee's marketing manager has estimated that 500 000 kg of implements will have to be transported to Ermelo each year for the next 5 years. The truck will be fully loaded each trip.

Taking into account the salvage value of the truck, it will be depreciated on a straight line basis over its useful life. This is also acceptable for tax purposes. Tax is levied at a rate of 40% p.a. The desired rate of return is 20% per year.

REQUIRED

1. Advise on the purchase of the truck. Use the Net Present Value technique.

2. Calculate the minimum number of trips per year that must be guaranteed by Camk to make the purchase acceptable to Mackee.

3. State and explain three qualitative factors that may influence the decision.

14 Financial Analysis

Having dealt with the components of financial statements and the management implications and aspects of various transactions, it is appropriate to give consideration to analysing financial statements and to examine the interrelationships of the figures disclosed.

Financial statements are often complex. They may contain so much information that 't may be difficult to assimilate and produce a meaningful overview. Ratio analysis facilitates interpretation of the financial statements by expressing selected figures or groups of figures in terms of their interrelationships. This assists the analyst to determine the position of a company and how it has been performing.

The Income Statement and Balance Sheet will be used to illustrate the calculation of some key ratios.

RATAN LTD
Income Statement for the year ended 31 December 02

	02 (R000's)	01 (R000's)
Turnover	1 500	1 350
Operating profit before the following items:	515	430
Audit fees	25	20
Interest paid	80	70
Depreciation	185	160
Lease premiums	25	30
	315	280
Net income before taxation	200	150
Taxation	80	60
Net income after taxation	120	90
Dividends paid	50	30
Retained income — for the year	70	60
— at the beginning of the year	180	120
— at the end of the year	250	180

RATAN LTD
Balance Sheet at 31 December 02

	02 (R000's)	01 (R000's)
Capital employed		
Share capital		
Authorised and issued R1 ordinary shares	600	600
Distributable reserve — retained income	250	180
Capital and reserves	850	780
Long term liabilities	725	620
	R1 575	R1 400
Employment of capital		
Fixed assets, book value	1 120	950
Current assets		
Stock	550	560
Accounts receivable	250	240
Cash resources	45	10
	845	810
Current liabilities		
Accounts payable	390	360
Working capital	455	450
	R1 575	R1 400

Given the large number of ratios that may be calculated, the user must decide what aspect of the business he wishes to investigate and which ratios are likely to be informative in this regard.

The more important areas for analysis are liquidity, asset management, leverage, and profitability.

LIQUIDITY

The ability of a business to meet its current obligations is an important aspect to examine. In this example Ratan Ltd has current assets of 845 and current liabilities of 390 and hence the ratio of current assets to current liabilities known as the current ratio is 2,2 [845 ÷ 390] and at the end of the previous year was 2,25 [810 ÷ 360] which indicates a marginal decrease in overall liquidity between the two year ends, i.e. current liabilities were covered 2,25 times and are now covered 2,2 times.

It is not the absolute figure which is important but the trend in the ratio which is the indicator of the direction in which the business is moving. It is therefore desirable to do the analysis using the figures for several years. For the purpose of illustration we will use the figures for the two years given in the example.

A further ratio to measure liquidity is the acid test or quick ratio. This ratio measures the ability of a business to meet its current obligations from its quick assets (cash and near cash assets). In other words the relationship of current assets other than stock to current liabilities.

Ratan Ltd has a quick ratio of 0,76 [(845 − 550) ÷ 390] which indicates that some of its stock must be sold before all the current obligations can be met from current assets.

At the previous year end the quick ratio was 0,69 [(810 − 560) ÷ 360] which indicates that although overall liquidity, as measured by the current ratio, has dropped slightly, the ability of the business to meet its current obligations from its quick asset resources has improved over the year.

ASSET MANAGEMENT

The amount of sales generated by assets, and more specifically, by fixed assets, indicates the efficiency with which management has utilised the assets at its disposal.

Ratan's fixed assets to turnover ratio (turnover ÷ fixed assets) has dropped from 1,4 times [1 350 ÷ 950] to 1,3 [1 500 ÷ 1 120] for the period under review, indicating that the assets have been slightly less efficiently used.

An evaluation of the management of debtors and stock is crucial to ascertain how these two important current assets are being controlled. This is particularly vital as the greater the amount of stock and accounts receivable held, the greater will be the cost of financing these two assets.

For this reason average number of days' accounts receivable are outstanding is measured. In the case of Ratan Ltd at 31/12/02 debtors are outstanding for an average of 60,8 days [250 ÷ 1 500 × 365] whereas this was 64,9 days [240 ÷ 1 350 × 365] at 31/12/01. this indicates improved management of accounts receivable.

In calculating the average number of days of stock-holding held, the most desirable basis of calculation would be to use the cost of sales to determine what proportion of this figure is represented by stock held. However, as this information is not usually made available in published financial statements, the denominator normally used is sales. As long as this is consistently applied it will remain a good trend indicator. In calculating this ratio the average stock-holding is sometimes used as the numerator but as long as a consistent basis is used, the ratio is an effective indication of the trend. In the case of Ratan Ltd at 31/12/01 it was 151,4 days [560 ÷ 1 350 × 365] while a year later it was 133,8 days [550 ÷ 1 500 × 365] which indicates that relative stock levels are being reduced. Whether or not this is desirable will depend on the nature of the business and the stock.

LEVERAGE

The risk profile of a business is an important factor to measure both in absolute and in trend terms. Although there are many other external factors which add to a business' risk profile, such as competition and the economic environment, the financial statements, if carefully analysed, can illustrate the immediate financial factors influencing the risk profile of the business. Leverage ratios, sometimes referred to as gearing ratios, can be useful indicators of risk profile.

The ability of a business to raise finance is an important factor. In general terms it can be said that lenders are prepared to lend a proportional amount to that which the owners of a business have themselves been prepared to invest. This proportion depends on the nature of the business.

The owners of the business will have injected funds by way of capital or share capital, and, in the case of a company, profits earned but not distributed to them by way of dividend. In the case of Ratan Ltd this amounts to 850 [600 + 250]. Creditors have injected accounts payable of 390 and long term liabilities of 725 and the ratio referred to as the debt:equity ratio is therefore 1,31 [(390 + 725) ÷ 850]. This indicates that the borrowing capacity may be limited unless the owners make a further capital investment. The debt raising capacity has dropped since 31/12/01 where the ratio was 1,26 [(360 + 620) ÷ 780].

A further consideration is that the company has leased certain assets, as indicated by lease premiums disclosed in the income statement. This means that the debt is understated. The net book value of the assets, which are the subject of the lease, is not disclosed and the liabilities are also understated as the liability to the lease creditor is undisclosed. In the case of leases where they are in effect simply a medium of financing the acquisition of assets, adjustment to the debt:equity ratio should be made on the basis outlined above.

In considering the questions of finance a factor to take into account is the cost of the finance. Broadly speaking the cost can be said to be either the interest cost in the case of most long term liabilities or the opportunity cost in the case of early payment discount foregone on trade credit when extended payment terms are utilised.

Where there is no question of discount, or the amount foregone by not taking discount on trade credit is less than the cost of other available forms of finance, trade credit can be the cheapest form of finance. The average number of days of trade credit used is a ratio that should be calculated.

This is most accurately calculated using cost of sales as the denominator. As mentioned in the case of the average number of days of stockholding, the cost of sales figure is not normally disclosed, instead the sales figure is often used. Consistent application of the numerator will meet the objective of it being a trend indicator. Bear in mind that accounts payable do not always relate only to stock purchases.

In the case of Ratan Ltd at 31/12/02 the average number of days of trade credit is 94,9 days [390 ÷ 1 500 × 365] and at 31/12/01 was 97,3 [360 ÷ 1 350 × 365] which indicates a shortening of the period. This may be questionable in the light of the debt:equity ratio trend but would be dependent on the considerations outlined above.

PROFITABILITY

Profitability can be measured by expressing net income after tax as a percentage of sales. The trend of this ratio over time, and with fluctuation in sales may give some indication of the effect of fixed costs on changes in volume. In the case of Ratan Ltd the ratio for the year ended 31/12/02 is 8% [120 ÷ 1 500 × 100] and for the year ended 31/12/01 was 6,7% [90 ÷ 1 350 × 100]. All things being equal it could be said that the increase in sales volume has resulted in a direct increase in contribution from those sales, but this may ignore the influence of other factors such as the effect of inflation or price cutting.

Gross profit expressed as a percentage of sales measures the consistency of mark up policies. It is a ratio which can only be calculated from internal information not normally contained in published financial statements. The qualifications made to the ratio of net income after tax to sales regarding other factors applies equally here.

A useful relationship to examine is the relationship of net income after taxation to assets. This, in the case of Ratan Ltd, is 6,1% [120 ÷ (845 + 1 120) × 100] for the year ended 31/12/02 and 5,1% [90 ÷ (810 + 950) × 100] for the year ended 31/12/01. This relationship is useful for illustrating the effectiveness of management, because the relationship can be broken down into:

$$\frac{\text{Income }\%}{\text{Assets}} = \frac{\text{Income }\%}{\text{Sales}} \times \frac{\text{Sales}}{\text{Assets}}$$

which shows how return on assets is a function of control over profit margins, and utilisation of assets.

In the case of Ratan Ltd this would be:

for the year ended 31/12/02:

$$\frac{120}{1\,965} \times 100 = \left[\frac{120}{1\,500} \times 100\right] \times \frac{1\,500}{1\,965}$$

i.e. 6,1% = 8% × 0,763

and for the year ended 31/12/01:

$$\frac{90}{1\,760} \times 100 = \left[\frac{90}{1\,350} \times 100\right] \times \frac{1\,350}{1\,760}$$

i.e. 5,1% = 6,7% × 0,767

This illustrates that sales per rand of assets utilised has dropped only marginally and that the increase in return has been generated almost entirely from income management.

USING RATIOS

Rules of thumb exist which state for example, that the current ratio should be 2, the quick ratio should be 1 and the debt equity ratio 1. These are only rules of thumb and the dangers associated with all generalisations exist. Ratios are particularly useful when used comparatively in one of the following ways:

— Trend analysis. The direction of movement of ratios provides valuable information. Listed companies usually provide ratios for periods of five to ten years.

— Industry averages. Information pertaining to other businesses in the same industry is useful particularly with regard to judging performance against industry averages, but with the qualification that no two companies can really be said to be truly comparable.

— Budgets and plans. For internal use it is particularly useful to evaluate the ratio against the objectives set for those indicators.

Ratio analysis can be a very useful tool to gain insight into the company, however, it should be used with care. The following are some important factors to be borne in mind when using ratios:

— The numerator and denominator should have a compatible relationship.

— The accounting policies adopted by a business will influence figures in its financial statements and hence the ratios calculated. For instance the method of valuing stock and periodic revaluation of some classes of fixed assets. While this will not have an effect on the trend indicated by the ratios (unless there has been a change in policy) it may have a marked effect in comparison to industry averages.

— The audit report, in the case of a company, should always be examined to ensure that no figures reported in the financial statements have been questioned by the auditors.

— Other components of the financial statements which may be provided, such as the directors' report, chairman's report, source and application of funds statement, the supplementary current cost income statement, the value added statement, and the notes to the financial statements should be referred to for information which may have a bearing on the analysis. An example of this is the disclosure of contingent liabilities and amounts contracted for relating to future capital expenditure.

— The year end may not be representative of the true nature of the financial position of the company. For example in seasonal business it makes sense to have the year end during the off-season. In such circumstances balance sheet ratios may be misleading.

— Many other factors such as environmental, geographic and economic factors may have a bearing on the business and these qualitative factors should be incorporated in the analysis.

Since most analysis is done in considering some course of action, it is imperative that factors which may have a future effect be taken into account. One of the single most important factors is the tax consequence not only for its effect on the profit of the business but also on the manner in which distributions are made to the shareholders.

SOURCE AND APPLICATION OF FUNDS

A component of the financial statements which was referred to earlier is the source and application of funds statement. This document shows in aggregate terms where the business raised its finance and how it has utilised that finance.

This statement based on the information in the example used in this chapter, would be as follows:

RATAN LTD

Statement of Source and Application of Funds
for the year ended 31 December 02

	(R000's)
Source of funds	
Net income before taxation	200
less: taxation	80
	120
add: amount not requiring the use of funds	
— depreciation	185
funds from operations	305
long term liabilities raised	105
	R410
Application of funds	
fixed assets acquired [1 120 + 185 − 950]	355
increase in working capital (see schedule)	5
dividends paid	50
	R410

Schedule of increase in working capital		
Increases		*(R000's)*
increase in accounts receivable		10
increase in cash resources held		35
		45
Decreases		
decrease in stock holding	10	
increase in accounts payable	30	40
Net increase in working capital		R5

The statement has shown that funds generated internally amounted to R305 (remember depreciation does not involve a flow of funds but is the amortisation of the cost of fixed assets, the purchase or sale of fixed assets would be the time when a flow of funds takes place) and that long term suppliers of credit advanced a net amount of R105.

The total amount raised has been shown as having been invested in fixed assets and the balance after paying a dividend of R50 was invested in working capital.

The statement of source and application of funds is therefore a summary of the cash flow for the year.

It is important to realise that a financial analysis of a business will only provide a numerical basis for a decision which in many cases may end up being fairly subjective. Although the figures are important they are not an end in themselves, they are pieces of information which help in arriving at a decision.

Perhaps it is appropriate to reiterate what was said in the preface to the first edition of this book, namely "... a little knowledge is a dangerous thing..."

QUESTIONS

14.1 Ratio analysis is not particularly useful unless the ratios of the business being analysed are viewed in relation to other ratios.

REQUIRED

To what other ratios should the business ratios be compared and explain how this is useful.

14.2 Eagle Ltd, a substantial listed company, is considering acquiring 100% of Hawk Ltd, another listed company in a similar line of business.

The management of Eagle believe that there are significant synergistic benefits to be derived from the acquisition but are not sure of the best way to fund the acquisition.

The options available to them are to fund the acquisition on one of the following bases:

1. Long term debt at 13% per annum,
2. the issue of ordinary shares at R2,00 each,
3. 50% debt and 50% by way of shares, in which case the cost of debt is expected to fall to 12,50%.

Eagle has currently got 200 million ordinary shares in issue and would have to maintain its dividend rate at 18 cents per share on its expanded capital in the event of funding through the issue of shares.

Hawk is expected to make profits of R45 million per annum and Eagle expects that the synergies of the acquisition will add R10 million to its own profits of R85 million.

What should the management of Eagle decide?

Assume that all interest cost is tax deductible, the profits referred to above are before tax at 40%, the acquisition will cost R230 million and all effects are for a full year.

14.3 The following are extracts from the annual financial statements of Sydcap:

Stock	10 000
Accounts receivable	20 000
Accounts payable	15 000
Bank overdraft	15 000
Sales	100 000
Cost of sales	60 000

Industry averages are:

Gross profit %	$33\frac{1}{3}$
Current ratio	1,5:1
Quick ratio	1:1
Days receivables outstanding	50 days
Stock turn	4 times

REQUIRED

Evaluate Sydcap's performance relative to the industry.